"Why should we know about texts once wrongly attributed to St. Bernard? The fact that some of them were extremely popular, while others were not or were in vogue only regionally suggests that readers looked beyond the *name* Bernard to the contents of the manuscripts. Lovingly translated and beautifully annotated, these works offer new and valuable glimpses into twelfth- and thirteenth-century religious mentalities."

— Barbara H. Rosenwein
Loyola University Chicago

"Like many great spiritual writers, Bernard of Clairvaux had a number of works pseudonymously ascribed to him after his death. In Bernard's case the total is said to be as high as 177. In modern times we rightly value authentic works over pseudonymous ones, but this should not lead us to neglect the 'pseudo-Bernard,' who has much to tell us about the saint's fame and the subsequent history of his ideas. This valuable translation provides readable and well-annotated versions of three pseudo-Bernardine meditative texts particularly useful for the religious formation of monks. It is a welcome addition to our knowledge of Bernard's afterlife and the history of the medieval monasticism."

— Bernard McGinn
Divinity School, University of Chicago

CISTERCIAN STUDIES SERIES: TWO HUNDRED SEVENTY-THREE

Three Pseudo-Bernardine Works

Translated and annotated by the *Catena Scholarium*
at the University of Notre Dame,
under the direction of
Ann W. Astell and Joseph Wawrykow,
with the assistance of Thomas Clemmons

With an Introduction by Dom Elias Dietz, OCSO

α

Cistercian Publications
www.cistercianpublications.org

LITURGICAL PRESS
Collegeville, Minnesota
www.litpress.org

A Cistercian Publications title published by Liturgical Press

Cistercian Publications
Editorial Offices
161 Grosvenor Street
Athens, Ohio 45701
www.cistercianpublications.org

BX
3402
.A2
T47
2018

The three Pseudo-Bernardine treatises in this volume are translated from the *Patrolgia Latina*, vol. 184:771–812, 1167–72.

Scripture texts in this work were translated by the members of the *Catena Scholarium*.

1   2   3   4   5   6   7   8   9

Library of Congress Control Number: 2017959765

ISBN 978-0-87907-173-8   ISBN 978-0-87907-573-6 (e-book)

Contents

Prefatory Acknowledgments

Catena Scholarium (Chain of Scholars) is a talented team of young translators and scholars at the University of Notre Dame who, under the direction of Ann W. Astell and Joseph Wawrykow, collectively undertake the ongoing work, semester by semester, of translating into English previously untranslated Latin theological writings. A conscious goal of the group is to expand the canon of medieval works available to present-day English readers.

The name *Catena Scholarium* recalls the famous *Catena Aurea* (1265) of Saint Thomas Aquinas, a compilatory commentary on the four gospels, but also the *Theologia Scholarium* (1140) of Peter Abelard. The word *catena* also has obvious biblical and hagiographic resonances, recalling, for example, the chain of the angel in Revelation 20:1-2, the chains of the prisoners Peter (Acts 12:6-7) and Paul (Eph 6:20), the virtuous *catena* of Catherine of Siena (used by her hagiographer, Raymond of Capua [1330–1399], to interpret her name, *Caterina* Benincasa), and the legendary chain with which Saint Bernard of Clairvaux (1090–1153) bound the devil. It bespeaks a bond of shared responsibility and cooperation between and among the interlinked members of the team.

More particularly, "Catena Scholarium" gives expression to the pedagogical method used to achieve the complete translation and annotation of the Pseudo-Bernardine essays in this volume. The individual graduate students who enrolled in the one-credit classes co-taught by Astell and Wawrykow in Fall 2014 and Spring 2015 each translated different short portions of the text weekly, as assigned on the syllabus. At the weekly meeting the preliminary translations were read aloud seriatim, corrected, and discussed. During the following week, the students submitted their revised and annotated translations to the group as a whole.

Throughout the process, the interpretive work of scholarly annotation went hand in hand with that of translation. In this regard, the identification of quoted and paraphrased biblical passages was important, but also that of parallel passages in patristic and medieval texts. Guiding questions for the group included the following: Why might this text have been attributed to Saint Bernard? Who wrote this treatise and when? For whom, for what sort of audience, was this treatise composed?

Selected students oversaw the compilation, section by section, of the individual contributions, which were then reviewed by the instructors and the class as a whole. The review process entailed not only addressing any remaining issues in grammar and style, but also identifying and highlighting the key Latin terms, theological themes, and logical distinctions that served to structure each treatise as a coherent composition.

The following students were members of the *Catena Scholarium* during one or more of the semesters devoted to work on the Pseudo-Bernardine writings: Margaret Blume, Gregory Cruess, Roberto De La Noval, Peter Freddoso, Maj-Britt Frenze, Mary Helen Gallucci-Wright, Joshua Lim, Alex C. J. Neroth van Vogelpoel, Breanna Nickel, Emily Nye, Nicholas Ogle, Jon Kara Shields, and Gilbert Stockson. Thomas Clemmons assisted in the work of instruction.

Commenting on the translated Pseudo-Bernardine texts on behalf of the whole team, Breanna Nickel and Gregory Cruess (substituting for Joshua Lim) presented papers in May 2017, alongside Dom Elias Dietz, OCSO, at a Cistercian Studies session moderated by Ann Astell at the International Congress on Medieval Studies at Western Michigan University. This volume, generously copyedited by Marsha Dutton and introduced by Dom Elias, brings the translated texts to a wider audience and demonstrates the value of studying the Pseudo-Bernardine texts both in their own right as historical witnesses and for the richly complex, formative contribution they have made to the tradition of Christian spirituality.

Every publication involves the work of many people, but this particular collection has been a team effort from the very start. The debt of mutual gratitude is great. Together with Joseph Wawrykow, I want to thank Dom Elias for first suggesting that we direct our efforts to some of the Pseudo-Bernardine treatises and especially

Marsha Dutton for her constant encouragement and patient editorial work. Finally, our thanks go to the staff at Liturgical Press for their expert engagement in seeing this project through to its completion.

Ann W. Astell
October 19, 2017

Translators and Annotators[1]

Formula honestae vitae: Instruction for the Honorable Life

¶ 1–4, Emily Nye

¶ 5–10, Joshua Lim

Instructio sacerdotalis. Instruction for a Priest:
A Treatise on the Principal Mysteries of Our Religion

Preface, Nicholas Ogle

¶ 1–6, Joshua Lim and Breanna Nickel

¶ 7–14, Maj–Britt Frenze and Peter Freddoso

¶ 15–25, Margaret Blume and Gilbert Stockson

¶ 26–32, Roberto De La Noval and Alex C. J. van Vogelpoel

¶ 33–36, Gregory Cruess

*Tractatus de statu virtutum humilitatis, obedientiae, timoris,
et charitatis.* A Treatise on the State of the Virtues

¶ 1–7, Peter Freddoso

¶ 8–15, Jon Kara Shields

¶ 16–19, Joshua Lim

¶ 20–24, Breanna Nickel

---

[1] All the members of the *Catena Scholarium* contributed to the translation and annotation of each section of the text, but the named individuals bore responsibility for the final smoothing and polishing of the compiled paragraphs.

Abbreviations

ASOC	*Analecta Sacri Ordinis Cisterciensis / Analecta Cisterciensia*. Rome, 1945– .
CCCM	Corpus Christianorum, Continuatio Mediaevalis. Turnhout: Brepols.
CCSL	Corpus Christianorum, Series Latina. Turnhout: Brepols.
CF	Cistercian Fathers series. Cistercian Publications.
CPL	Clavis Patrum Latinorum
CS	Cistercian Studies series. Cistercian Publications.
CSQ	*Cistercian Studies Quarterly*
DSpir	*Dictionnaire de Spiritualité*
Ep(p)	Epistola(e)
Ep Frat	William of Saint-Thierry. *Epistola (aurea) ad fratres de Monte Dei*. Ed. Paul Verdeyen. CCCM 88. Turnhout: Brepols, 2003.
FC	Fathers of the Church. 127 vols. Washington, DC: The Catholic University Press.
Fry	*RB 1980: The Rule of St. Benedict in Latin and English with Notes*. Ed. Timothy Fry. Collegeville, MN: Liturgical Press, 1981.
Gen ad litt	Augustine. *De Genesi ad litteram libri duodecim*.
Hesbert	René-Jean Hesbert. *Antiphonale Missarum sextuplex*. Bruxelles: Vromant, 1935.

MGH auct. ant.	Monumenta Germaniae Historica. Auctores antiquissimi.
Moralia	Gregory the Great, *Moralia in Iob.* Ed. Marc Adriaen. CCSL 143, 143A, 143B. Turnhout: Brepols, 1979.
NPNF	Library of the Nicene and Post-Nicene Fathers of the Christian Church. Ed. Philip Schaff and Henry Wace.
PL	Patrologiæ cursus completus, series latina. Ed. J.-P. Migne. 221 volumes. Paris, 1844–1864.
RBen	*Revue bénédictine.* Maredsous, Belgium, 1884– .
RHE	*Revue d'histoire ecclésiastique.* Louvain (Belgium), 1900– .
S(s)	Sermon(s)
SBOp	Sancti Bernardi Opera. Ed. J. Leclercq, H. M. Rochais, C. H. Talbot. Rome: Cistercienses, 1957–1977.
SS ref. Germ.	Scriptores Rerum Germanicarum. Monumenta Germania Historica.
ST	Thomas Aquinas. *Summa Theologica.*
Symb Athan	Athanasian Creed

Works of Bernard of Clairvaux

Apo	*Apologia ad Guillelmum abbatem.* SBOp 3:61–108; "*St Bernard's Apologia to Abbot William.*" Translated by Michael Casey. In The Works of Bernard of Clairvaux, 1, Treatises I. CF 1. Spencer, MA, and Shannon, Ireland: Cistercian Publications, 1970.
Csi	*De consideratione.* SBOp 3:379–493; *Five Books on Consideration: Advice to a Pope.* Translated by John D. Anderson and Elizabeth T. Kennan. Bernard of Clairvaux, vol. 13. CF 37. Kalamazoo, MI: Cistercian Publications, 1976.

Dil	*Liber de diligendo Deo.* SBOp 3:109–54; *On Loving God.* Translated by Robert Walton. CF 13B. Kalamazoo, MI: Cistercian Publications, 1995.
Div	*Sermones Diversis.* SBOp 6:56–406; *Monastic Sermons.* Translated by Daniel Griggs. CF 68. Collegeville, MN: Cistercian Publications, 2016.
Gra	*De gratia et libero arbitrio.* SBOp 3:155–203; *On Grace and Free Choice.* Translated by Daniel O'Donovan. In *Bernard of Clairvaux, Treatises III.* CF 19. Kalamazoo, MI: Cistercian Publications, 1977. 3–111.
Hum	*Liber de gradibus humilitatis et superbiæ.* SBOp 3:13–59. "The Steps of Humility and Pride." In *Bernard of Clairvaux, Treatises II.* Translated by M. Ambrose Conway. CF 13. Kalamazoo, MI: Cistercian Publications, 1980. 1–82.
Miss	*Homiliae super "Missus est" in Laudibus Virginis Matris.* SBOp 4:3–58; *Magnificat: Homilies in Praise of the Blessed Virgin Mary.* Translated by Marie-Bernard Saïd. CF 18. Kalamazoo, MI: Cistercian Publications, 1979. 1–58.
Mor	*Ep de moribus et officiis episcoporum* (Ep 42). SBOp 7:100–31; *On Baptism and the Office of Bishops.* Translated by Pauline Matarasso. CF 67. Kalamazoo, MI: Cistercian Publications, 2004.
SC	Sermo super Cantica canticorum: SBOp 1–2; CF 4, 7, 31, 40.
Tpl	*Liber ad milites templi (De laude novæ militiæ).* SBOp 3:205–39; "In Praise of the New Knighthood." Translated by Daniel O'Donovan. In *The Works of Bernard of Clairvaux*, vol. 7, *Treatises III.* CF 19. Kalamazoo, MI: Cistercian Publications, 1977. 113–67.

Introduction

The three works presented here in English translation belong to a category of writings that has received relatively little attention in recent decades. In order to place these three items in a meaningful context, it seems best to begin with an overview of the Pseudo-Bernardine writings and of the major questions raised by these kinds of texts. Specific introductions for each of the three works will then follow.

The Real Bernard and the Pseudo-Bernard

A whole generation has now benefited from the publication of Saint Bernard's works in the critical edition prepared by Jean Leclercq and Henri Rochais in the 1950s.[1] Readers who use that edition or translations made from it are confident that all of the texts included there are authentically Bernardine. And thanks to this confidence about what Bernard wrote and didn't write, the many texts once attributed to him are generally set aside as inauthentic and un-important. From a historical perspective, though, this is a new and unusual state of affairs. It is also a mistake.

For one thing, the distinction authentic/inauthentic is not black and white within the recognized Bernardine corpus. To call a work genuinely "Bernardine" does not necessarily mean that every word of every text was composed by Bernard. There are grey areas between the various degrees of authenticity. Secretaries were involved at different stages of writing, and some texts have the character of mere outlines or summaries of teaching delivered orally. In sorting out

---

[1] Sancti Bernardi Opera (Rome: Editiones Cistercienses, 1957) (=SBOp).

these texts, the editors of the critical edition encountered some surprises. Only in the face of overwhelming evidence did Leclercq and Rochais come to accept the authenticity of certain *De Diversis* sermons and *Sentences*, some of which seem no more worthy of that distinction than most Pseudo-Bernard works.[2] Moreover, early on in the manuscript tradition, apocryphal works appeared mixed in with genuine ones. As time went on, Bernard's fame created a kind of gravitational pull, making it more and more likely for scribes to put things under his name deliberately or out of ignorance or as an educated guess. Some Pseudo-Bernard works were more successful than most of the authentic works, as was the case with the *Meditationes*, copied in over six hundred manuscripts and constantly reprinted into the nineteenth century.[3] Copyists and editors were eager to collect anything with Saint Bernard's name on it. A good witness of this trend is Bernard Tissier, prior of the Cistercian abbey Bonnefontaine and one of the consultants for Jean Mabillon's first edition of Bernard's collected works (1667). In 1662, he wrote,

> If I were to undertake this project, I would proceed in a manner exactly opposite from the one that has prevailed up to the present, and I would completely remove from these works anything that is not Saint Bernard's, instead of, with every new edition, giving him a few new pieces of which he is not at all the author.[4]

This question of sorting out the genuine and apocryphal works was the biggest challenge for Mabillon. It is significant to note that, notwithstanding Mabillon's general concern regarding authenticity,

---

[2] For further information and bibliography on the question of authenticity, see Jean Leclercq, "Introduction to Saint Bernard's Sermons *De diversis*," CSQ 42 (2007): 37–41; and Jean Leclercq, "Introduction to the *Sentences* of Bernard of Clairvaux," CSQ 46 (2011): 277–86.

[3] For an extensive history of this text and for a comprehensive study of the phenomenon of pseudepigraphic texts, see Cédric Giraud, *Spiritualité et histoire des textes entre Moyen Âge et époque moderne. Genèse et fortune d'un corpus pseudépigraphe de méditations*, Série Moyen Âge et Temps Modernes 52 (Paris: Institut d'Études Augustiniennes, 2016).

[4] Jean Leclercq, "La préhistoire de l'édition de Mabillon," in *Études sur Saint Bernard et le texte de ses écrits*, ASOC 9 (1953): 202–25, here 207.

he nonetheless opted to include an entire volume of *Opera dubia, notha et supposititia* (dubious, spurious, and inauthentic works). Tissier had done the groundwork for Mabillon, sorting out these texts and assigning them to their true authors where possible. But removing them from the collection of Bernard's works did not mean discarding them altogether. Tissier, after all, had compiled his own *Library of Cistercian Fathers*[5] and was eager to make known the writings of Bernard's Cistercian contemporaries as well as works from the following generation. So a number of misattributed and anonymous works were also included in this appendix to Mabillon's edition. The inclusion of works like Gilbert of Hoyland's *Sermons on the Song of Songs* and William of Saint-Thierry's *Golden Epistle* was a way of definitively remedying these serious misattributions and of promoting these texts under their true author's name. As for the texts of doubtful or unidentifiable authorship, few reasons are given for including them in the collection. Some are provided with a brief introduction or explanatory footnote; some appear without comment. No doubt these items were judged to come from manuscripts of value. Perhaps Mabillon's characterization of the first two and best-known items of this category reveal something of his rationale for editing the whole: the *Meditationes* "are not Bernard's but are not unworthy of him," and the *De interiori domo* is a "pious and useful work" by one of his Cistercian contemporaries.[6]

The Intrinsic Value of the Pseudepigraphical Works

On one hand it is understandable that Pseudo-Bernardine works have been relegated to the background over the last few centuries. Increased historical consciousness brings with it greater sensitivity to questions of authenticity, especially in the case of someone like Bernard of Clairvaux, whose image was shaped (or misshaped) by the popularity of the apocryphal works under his name throughout

[5] The complete title of Tissier's 1660 edition reads, *Bibliotheca Patrum Cisterciensium. Opera abbatum et monachorum ordinis Cisterciensis, qui saeculo S. Bernardi, aut paulo post eius obitum floruerunt.*

[6] Since these same introductions appear in all the editions, the simplest reference is to Migne's Patrologia Latina: for the *Meditationes,* see PL 184:485–86; for *De interiori domo,* see PL 184:507–8.

the Middle Ages and well into modern times. It is an advantage to have an accurate list of works and reliable biographical documentation for so central a figure. On the other hand, it seems that the time has come to retrieve some of the "pious and useful" material that falls under the umbrella of Pseudepigraphical works. A parallel might be drawn with the revival of interest in Cistercian *exempla* in recent years, which has resulted in important new editions and translations.[7] Compared to the writings of figures like William, Bernard, or Aelred, these stories are secondary in terms of both substance and style. They are, nevertheless, rich in real-life details and lived experience that not only complement our information about the material culture and mentalities of the period but also paint a lively picture of how Cistercian men and women both failed and succeeded in living out their values and religious aspirations. A comparable revival of interest in Pseudepigraphical texts would bring similar benefits. As Mark DelCogliano has said regarding the minor authors of what he calls the Silver Age,

> Cistercians of the late twelfth and early thirteenth centuries were very much aware that previous generations of Cistercians had bequeathed to them a vast corpus of spiritual writings that merited study and application. In their era, there was no need to try to repeat their achievement but rather to interpret it and re-express it, in a way that would help ordinary monks live their day-to-day lives. In other words, Cistercian monks of the late twelfth and early thirteenth centuries needed the writings of the earlier Cistercian Fathers translated into practical terms. Earlier Cistercians had expressed the theory, or perhaps the theology, of Cistercian spirituality, and subsequent Cistercians felt the need to articulate its practice.[8]

---

[7] For an overview of this development, see Brian Patrick McGuire, "Cistercian Storytelling—A Living Tradition: Surprises in the World of Research," CSQ 39 (2004): 281–309; the most important translation of such works in recent years is Benedicta Ward and Paul Savage, trans., E. Rozanne Elder, ed., *The Great Beginning of Cîteaux: A Narrative of the Beginning of the Cistercian Order: the Exordium Magnum of Conrad of Eberbach*, CF 72 (Collegeville, MN: Cistercian Publications, 2012).

[8] Mark DelCogliano, "Cistercian Monasticism in the Silver Age: Two Texts on Practical Advice," CSQ 45 (2010): 421–52.

The Historical Importance of the Pseudo-Bernard Writings

This work of interpretation, application, and re-expression had the added benefit of making these texts quite accessible. Anonymity afforded the writers greater freedom of expression in presenting traditional material in an experiential, personal key. Their intended audience may have been monks or perhaps novices, but the works themselves ended up reaching secular clergy and educated lay persons as well. Works of this kind were particularly conducive to meditative reading, and, as Cédric Giraud has shown, their popularity came to shape the meaning of the word *meditation* in the West.[9] Another key concept shaped by these works is *conscience*.[10] According to Mirko Breitenstein, they popularized the twelfth century's new ethic of conviction (*Gesinnungsethik*) and thus conveyed into modern times a notion of conscience that has to do not only with fear and uncertainty about salvation but also with freedom, self-determination, and responsibility.[11]

Of particular importance is the role these texts played in medieval formation practices.[12] Some Pseudo-Bernardine works were specifically intended for novices, others served as sources for these kinds of writings, and several became standard novitiate reading. A few selections from this literature have been the object of editions and translations in recent years, and the present volume includes three such texts. The far-reaching influence of these kinds of works is illustrated in a thirteenth-century reading list for Dominican novices (by Master General Humbert of Romans, †1277), which recommends the following:

[9] Giraud, *Spiritualité et histoire*, 37–117.

[10] Philippe Delhaye, "Dans le sillage de S. Bernard. Trois petits traités *De Conscientia*," *Cîteaux* 5 (1954): 92–103.

[11] Mirko Breitenstein, "Der Tracktat 'Vom inneren Haus.' Verantwortung als Ziel der Gewissensbuildung," in *Innovation in Klöstern und Orden des Hohen Mittelalters: Aspekte und Pragmatik eines Begriffs*, ed. Mirko Breitenstein, Stefan Burkhardt, and Julia Burkhardt, Vita regularis 48 (Berlin: LIT, 2012), 263.

[12] Mirko Breitenstein, *Das Noviziat im hohen Mittelalter: Zur Organisation des Eintrittes bei den Cluniazensern, Cisterziensern und Franziskanern*, Vita regularis 38 (Münster: LIT, 2009), 29–33, where further bibliography is found.

Hugh's *De disciplina,* the book *De claustro animae,* Bl. Bernard's *Meditationes,* Anselm's *Meditationes* and *Orationes,* Augustine's *liber Confessionum,* along with the *Abbreviata* and *Florigerus* from Augustine, the *Collationes, Vitae,* and *Dicta* of the [desert] Fathers, the *Passiones* and *Legendae Sanctorum,* Bernard's *Epistola ad Fratres de Monte Dei,* the book *De gradibus superbiae,* the *Liber Barlaam,* the *Tractatus de vitiis et virtutibus,* and other similar works.[13]

Looking further afield, it should be noted that Bernard—and just as often, Pseudo-Bernard—appealed to a broad spectrum of sensitivities. Both his authentic and his apocryphal works were appreciated by adherents to the movement known as *Devotio Moderna.*[14] Through that movement Pseudo-Bernardine works influenced spirituality in the West into modern times through *The Imitation of Christ,* whose author drew freely on them. Bernard's name and the special character of these works also made it possible for them to cross denominational lines. Luther's admiration for Bernard ensured that certain of his works or works attributed to him had a place in the libraries of the reformers. Thanks largely to its attribution to Bernard, a minor work in verse by a thirteenth-century Cistercian entitled *Rythmus ad singula membra Christi patentis* had a remarkable future through Paul Gerhardt's translation of it into German, which in turn was used for the hymn "O Haupt voll Blut und Wunden," first published in 1656, often referred to as the "Passion Chorale" ("O Sacred Head Surrounded" in a later, Catholic version).[15] Parts of the original Latin text were set to music by Dietrich Buxtehude in his 1680 cycle of cantatas entitled *Membra Jesu nostri* (BuxWV 75), which continues to be performed and recorded today.

No doubt the lesser of these works only survive because of their association with Bernard. In the case of the more important ones, though, the Pseudo-Bernardine attribution is only one factor in their success. The only way to know the historical Bernard of Clairvaux

---

[13] Cited in Giraud, *Spiritualité et histoire,* 34.

[14] Giraud, *Spiritualité et histoire,* 270–75.

[15] For a full account of this hymn's long history, see George Faithful, "A More Brotherly Song, a Less Passionate Passion: Abstraction and Ecumenism in the Translation of the Hymn 'O Sacred Head Now Wounded' from Bloodier Antecedents," *Church History* 82 (2013): 779–811.

is to set aside all the apocryphal texts. But the only way to understand the Bernard of history as he was known from the thirteenth through the nineteenth centuries is take these texts into account.

Toward a Canon of Pseudo-Bernard Works

If the task of establishing the authentic corpus of Bernard's writings is one of elimination, any attempt at recovering the most important Pseudo-Bernardine texts will necessarily involve selection. In his 1891 *Bibliographia Bernardina*, Leopold Janauschek listed 177 works falsely attributed to Saint Bernard, 120 of them in prose and 57 in verse.[16] Ferdinand Cavallera's 1935 article on these apocrypha provides an initial sorting-out of this unwieldy and disparate body of texts.[17] His division of them into three categories—extracts or abridged versions of authentic works, works restored to their true authors, and apocryphal works by unknown authors—is a first step toward reducing the list to a manageable number. His attributions, however, must be used with caution, since subsequent scholarship has made several additions and corrections.

Because a number of these works circulated under more than one name, the effort to sort out the Bernardine apocrypha overlaps in many cases with similar tasks regarding other authors, especially Saint Augustine and Hugh of Saint Victor.[18] Other important resources for this effort are studies of *florilegia*,[19] of devotional texts,[20]

---

[16] Leopold Janauschek, *Bibliographia Bernardina qua Sancti Bernardi primi abbatis Claravallensis operum cum omnium tum singulorum editiones ac versiones, vitas et tractatus de eo scriptos quotquot usque ad finem anni MDCCCXC reperire potuit*, Xenia Bernardina 4 (Vienna: Hölder, 1891), IV–XIV.

[17] Ferdinand Cavallera, "Bernard (Apocryphes attribués à saint)," DSpir 1:1499–1502.

[18] See especially Patrice Sicard, Iter victorinum. *La tradition manuscrite des œuvres de Hugues et de Richard de Saint-Victor. Répertoire complémentaire et études*, Biblioteca Victorina 24 (Turnhout: Brepols, 2015).

[19] Mary A. Rouse and Richard H. Rouse, *Preachers, Florilegia and Sermons: Studies on the* Manipulus florum *of Thomas of Ireland* (Toronto: PIMS, 2000).

[20] Thomas H. Bestul, *Texts of the Passion: Latin Devotional Literature and Medieval Society* (Philadelphia: University of Pennsylvania Press, 2015).

and of treatises on the virtues and vices.[21] Strictly speaking, very few of the Pseudo-Bernardine works fall into this latter category,[22] but Morton Bloomfield's *Incipits of Latin Works on the Virtues and Vices, 1100–1500 A.D.*—along with the 2008 *Supplement* to that work—remains an indispensable starting point for tracing the manuscript tradition of these texts.

In the end, as was the case in Mabillon's appendix to Bernard's *Opera omnia*, there are no obvious objective criteria for deciding which texts are worth editing, translating, and studying. Since very few of them have been the object of critical editions, a great deal of work remains to be done. Without such editions, many questions of date and authorship will remain unanswered. In the meantime, translation efforts like the present volume, even if based on old editions, are a good, if provisional, step forward. The texts that deserve priority treatment are anonymous Cistercian works or works of uncertain attribution that date from the twelfth and thirteenth centuries. Nearly all the sermons included in Mabillon's appendix can be attributed to a known author. The remaining works fall more or less into four categories. A first group, the *De conscientia* treatises, are a kind of experiential counterpart to *De anima* works. Highly introspective in character, these texts are meant to encourage the moral reform of the person from within. A second group consists of short works of practical advice or so-called *mirrors*, some of which are intended for novices. Various meditations on the passion form a third group. And, finally, there are devotional texts in the form of prayers or hymns.

The following list is offered as a first attempt at forming a canon of worthwhile texts from these categories. This list is limited to items edited in Mabillon's edition, but it is possible that worthwhile texts are to be located among some of the unedited works listed by Janauschek. Titles and column numbers are given as found in

---

[21] Morton W. Bloomfield, *Incipits of Latin Works on the Virtues and Vices, 1100–1500 A.D.: Including a Section of Works on the Pater Noster* (Cambridge, MA: The Medieval Academy of America, 1979); Richard Newhauser and István Bejczy, *A Supplement to Morton W. Bloomfield et al., Incipits of Latin Works on the Virtues and Vices, 1100–1500 A.D.* (Turnhout: Brepols, 2008).

[22] Richard Newhauser, *The Treatise on Vices and Virtues in Latin and the Vernacular* (Turnhout: Brepols, 1993), 55–96.

volume 184 of the Patrologia Latina. Where possible their number in Bloomfield's repertory is also noted.

De Conscientia treatises:

Meditationes piissimae de cognitione humanae conditionis; col. 485–508; Bloomfield 3126.[23]

De interiori Domo, seu de Consciencia aedificanda; col. 507–52; Bloomfield 1787.

De Conscientia; col. 551–60; Bloomfield 3896.

Short works of practical advice or so-called mirrors:

Formula honestae vitae; col. 1167–72; Bloomfield 3897.

Tractatus de statu virtutum humilitatis, obedientiae, timoris, et charitatis; col. 791–812; Bloomfield 0740.

Speculum monachorum; col. 1175–78; Bloomfield 5582.

Doctrina Sancti Bernardi; col. 1177–82.

Octo puncta Perfectionis assequendae; col. 1181–86; Bloomfield 2303.

Meditations on the passion:

Lamentatio in Passionem Christi; col. 769–72.[24]

Rhythmus ad singula membra Christi patientis; col. 1319–24.

Devotional texts:

Jubilus Rhythmicus de Nomine Jesu; col. 1317–20.[25]

---

[23] For a summary of the manuscript history of this text, see Giraud, *Spiritualité et histoire*, 476–77.

[24] On the importance of the *Lamentatio*, see Charlotte Allen, "Thirteenth-Century English Religious Lyrics, Religious Women, and the Cistercian Imagination," PhD dissertation, Catholic University of America, 2011, 140–41.

[25] This is the hymn "Iesu, dulcis memoria," often attributed to Bernard but probably the work of an anonymous thirteenth-century Cistercian. For an edition and study of the text, see André Wilmart, *Le Jubilus Dit de Saint Bernard*, Storia e Letteratura 2 (Rome: Edizioni di Storia et Letteratura, 1944).

Conclusion

The fact that Pseudo-Bernardine works were popular and accessible in the Middle Ages is no guarantee that they will appeal to a modern audience. Readers familiar with early Cistercian authors will be at home in some passages. Other passages will seem quite foreign to them, but that foreignness itself is instructive about the cultural shifts to which these works bear witness. Jean Leclercq's quip about one of the texts translated in this volume will no doubt apply in many cases: "The main value of such apocryphal works is not that they show Bernard's influence . . . but that, by contrast, they make us appreciate the real Bernard even more."[26]

It is now time to introduce the three selections translated in this volume. They are fairly representative of the kinds of works discussed in this general introduction. All are short works of instruction. One was intended for novices and another no doubt became standard reading for novices. Two were originally anonymous texts that only later fell under Bernard's wide umbrella. The authorship of one is perhaps a case of mistaken identity, but its correct attribution is far from certain. Two of them attest to the fact that the authors of Pseudo-Bernardine works borrowed from each other or else used common sources that have since been lost. They range from well known and often copied to little known and seldom copied. And no doubt readers' response to them will range from delight to dismay.

Formula honestae vitae.
Instruction for the Honorable Life[27]

This brief text is ideal for a first contact with the Pseudo-Bernardine works of the Silver Age. Although it belongs to the category of short treatises of practical advice, its emphasis on the world of the thoughts

---

[26] The text in question is the third in this volume, "De Statu Virtutum." Jean Leclercq, "Le premier traité authentique de Saint Bernard?" RHE 48 (1953): 196–210, here 210; reprinted in Jean Leclercq, *Recueil d'études sur saint Bernard et ses écrits* (Rome: Edizioni di Storia e Letteratura, 1966), 2:51–68, here 67.

[27] PL 184:1167–72; Bloomfield (and Supplement) 3897; see also Sicard, Iter victorinum, 604–11.

and the movements of the heart creates an atmosphere similar to that of the *De conscientia* treatises. Not only does it recommend introspection and self-knowledge, but it is also composed in such a way that the act of reading it leads the reader into an experience of interiority. Its combination of an optimistic, encouraging tone with challenging moral demands places it firmly in the tradition of early Cîteaux. The author is steeped in the best of Cistercian literature: the method of engaging the memory and senses in meditation on biblical scenes is reminiscent of Aelred, Bernard's influence can be seen in the use of passages from the Song of Songs, and the importance given to recalling the events of the passion is typical of the *memoria passionis* so often recommended by these same authors. The composite nature of the text, with two apparently borrowed passages tacked on at the end, also places it in the lineage of anonymous works of the Silver Age. In some respects the *Formula honestae vitae* is reminiscent of writings intended specifically for novices, like the *Mirror for Novices*, a longer and probably contemporary work written in England. The scenario is clearly that of an experienced monk giving advice to a less experienced monk, but nothing in the work indicates that the advice is being given to a novice.

As is the case with many Pseudepigraphical works, this one goes by a number of titles[28] and is sometimes attributed to other authors, in this case, Hugh of Saint Victor. It is important not to mistake its *incipit* ("Petis a me, frater carissime") with the similar *incipit* of the treatise *De conscientia* ("Petis a me, dilecte mi"). Confusion must also be avoided between this *Formula honestae vitae* and a work with the same title by Martin of Braga.[29] The popularity of *Formula honestae vitae* is attested by over seventy surviving manuscript witnesses, a number that will probably increase with further inquiry. It is no surprise that one of the variant titles calls it a *speculum*, since it is similar to the *Speculum monachorum* in length, content, and tone.[30] It

---

[28] E.g., *Speculum beati Bernardi abbatis de honestate vitae, De modo conversandi, Tractatus de formula vitae sive de novitiis.*

[29] For bibliography on Martin of Braga's work, see Patrice Sicard, Iter victorinum, 604, n. 17.

[30] The *Speculum monachorum* is sometimes ascribed to Arnulf of Bohéries, although there remain many mysteries about identity of this Arnulf and as many

also shares with that work nearly word for word a remarkable passage entitled "A Useful Admonition about the Consideration of Death," although it seems to be an add-on. There is also some overlap between the *Formula honestae vitae* and yet another Pseudo-Bernard work entitled *Octo puncta Perfectionis assequendae*.[31] The relationship between these works is a puzzle that will only be resolved when there are critical editions of all three. In the meantime it is impossible to say which borrows from which.[32]

Instructio sacerdotalis.
Instruction for a Priest:
A Treatise on the Principal Mysteries of Our Religion[33]

The organization of this *Instructio* is fairly simple. The author is responding to a friend's question about the mystery of what takes place at Mass:

> Your intention, unless I am mistaken, was for it to be explained to you, by genuine authorities and suitable examples, in what way Christ, although on the altar he is hidden and veiled beneath the species of bread, nevertheless remains in the splendor of infinite and inestimable clarity.

Rather than address the question straightaway, the author chooses to respond by providing an ample theological framework. He divides the work into three parts, each part dealing with one of three gifts of Christ (or one threefold gift): "First, that the Son of God, dying

---

doubts about the authorship of that work. For a recent study and edition of this text, see Mirko Breitenstein, "*Consulo tibi speculum monachorum*. Geschichte und Rezeption eines pseudo-bernhardinischen Traktates (mit vorläufiger Edition)," *Revue Mabillon* 20 (2009): 113–49; for a recent translation of this text, see Mark DelCogliano, "Cistercian Monasticism," 437–40.

[31] This text is also introduced and translated in Mark DelCogliano, "Cistercian Monasticism," 429–35 and 441–51.

[32] On this bibliographical wasp's nest, see István Bejczy, "De 'Formula vitae honestae' in het Middelnederlands: een bibliografisch wespennest," *Ons Geestelijk Erf* 78 (2004): 25–30; and Breitenstein, *Consulo tibi*, 121–22 and 126–27.

[33] PL 184:771–92.

for us, gave himself to us; second, that he gives himself to us in the Eucharist; third, that he gives himself to us in eternal life." The central question about the Eucharist is thus framed by consideration of the Lord's self-giving in this life (the incarnation and passion) and his self-gift as our reward in heaven.

Perhaps because of its theological approach, the *Instructio* was the object of a partial English translation, published in 1954, under the title *The Threefold Gift of Christ*,[34] thus receiving a degree of attention unusual for most Pseudo-Bernardine works. In addition to making minor omissions in the text, this translation leaves out nearly all of part three, where it is a question of hell, because, as the translator saw it, "the crude realism of the mediaeval approach to that subject does not commend itself to modern minds" (*Threefold Gift*, 6). So this new translation is a useful contribution not only because it includes the entire text but also because of its extensive annotations dealing with vocabulary, sources, comparisons with contemporary works, and other background information.

This *Instructio* goes by more than one name and is often called *De praecipuis mysteriis nostrae religionis*,[35] so the translators do well to combine the titles. The association of this work with Bernard of Clairvaux is probably a case of mistaken identity. Its *incipit*, "Reverendo sacerdoti, Frater Bernardus," led scribes to assign it to the Bernard they knew best. A more likely author is a certain Bernardus Cluniensis (or Cluniacensis), perhaps the Cluniac Prior Bernard of Morlax.[36] This Cluniac Bernard was a prolific writer of poetry, and a number of works in verse from the mid-twelfth century can confidently be attributed to him. Whether or not this same Bernard of Morlax wrote the *Instructio sacerdotalis* is still an open question. The most that can be said is that, on the basis of a careful comparison between the

---

[34] The full title of this translation by Ruth Penelope Lawson is *The Threefold Gift of Christ. By Brother Bernard. Translated and Edited by a Religious of C.S.M.V. (i.e. Sister Penelope) [A Translation of "Instructio Sacerdoti de Praecipuis Mysteriis Nostrae Religionis," Formerly Attributed to St. Bernard of Clairvaux]*, Fleur de Lys Series of Spiritual Classics 4 (London: Mowbray, 1954).

[35] Other titles used are *Epistola beati Bernardi ad sacerdotem* and *Gemma crucifixi*.

[36] The name of the place of this Bernard's monastery is found in many forms: Morlaas, Morlaix, Morlas, or Morval; see André Wilmart, "Grands poèmes inédits de Bernard le clunisien," RBen 45 (1933): 249.

Instructio and the few prose passages known to have been written by this Bernard, there are no grounds to deny him authorship of this work.[37] This case is a good illustration of the difficulties involved in sorting out the origins of the mass of writings under the all-too-general designation Pseudo-Bernard.

To judge by the relatively small number of extant manuscript witnesses (twelve), the *Instructio* seems to have enjoyed only a modest dissemination. The manuscript tradition also indicates that this work was distributed mostly in Germanic lands, which is another reason for caution regarding its attribution to the prior of a Cluniac house in France. It circulated most often with other works on the liturgy or with collections of like-minded material intended to promote reform of the clergy.

De statu virtutum humilitatis, obedientiae, timoris, et charitatis. A Treatise on the State of the Virtues[38]

This treatise exemplifies many of the typical aspects of anonymous Pseudo-Bernardine works. The author's inspiration clearly comes from genuine works of Bernard of Clairvaux, but in some instances the writer of this text displays a less-than-perfect grasp of the original Bernard's thoughts. As is stated at its outset, the work is intended "for the growth of novices," and its accessibility apparently gained for it an even wider audience. The relative popularity of the piece is attested by over twenty extant manuscripts, originating mostly from Germanic regions. Another indication of its widespread distribution is the fact that it is used as one of the sources for a work entitled *De novitiis instruendis*, a late-twelfth-century Cluniac text consisting mostly of citations from patristic and monastic sources.[39] The textual

---

[37] Francis John Balnaves, "Bernard of Morlaix: The Literature of Complaint, the Latin Tradition and the Twelfth-century 'Renaissance,'" PhD thesis, Australian National University, March 1997, 15–16.

[38] PL 184:791–812; Bloomfield 0740.

[39] Mirko Breitenstein, De novitiis instruendis: *Text und Kontext eines anonymen Traktates vom Ende des 12. Jahrhunderts*, Vita regularis 1 (Münster: LIT, 2004), 60–61.

history of this *Treatise on the State of the Virtues* is complicated by the fact that it circulated in two forms: most of the extant copies carry a long version of the text, but about one quarter of them carry a shorter text.[40]

This twelfth-century treatise had an unexpected day in court in the mid-twentieth century. At that time, the chronology of the earliest writings of Bernard of Clairvaux was in full debate. In 1950, George B. Burch built an interesting case, arguing not only that the section on humility in *A Treatise on the State of the Virtues* was an authentic work by Bernard of Clairvaux but also that this *De humilitate* (*On Humility*)—as Bernard refers to it in his *Letter 18*—was his first published work, and not the *De gradibus humilitatis* (*On the Steps of Humility*).[41] Jean Leclercq, at the time fully engaged in preparatory work for the critical edition of Bernard's writings, had the means at hand to investigate the value of Burch's claim. As Leclercq argued in a 1953 article, the manuscript tradition of the *Treatise on the State of the Virtues* indicates that it is a unified composition and does not support the hypothesis of an independent existence of the section on humility in *De gradibus*. Moreover, careful analysis of the text reaffirms that the section on humility was written by the same author as the rest of the work. Finally, the differences in style and thought make an attribution of this text to Bernard of Clairvaux unthinkable. Thanks to Burch's hypothesis and Leclercq's refutation, we are better informed about this treatise than we are about most Pseudo-Bernardine works. No author can be named, but, as Leclercq shows, there is good reason to assign it to a twelfth-century Cistercian, who, according to a note in one manuscript, may have been an abbot.

Dom Elias Dietz, OCSO

---

[40] For a detailed account of the manuscript tradition of this text, see Jean Leclercq, "Le premier traité," 196–210 (RHE); 196–210 (Recueil).

[41] George B. Burch, *The Steps of Humility by Bernard, Abbot of Clairvaux*, 3d ed. (Cambridge, MA: Harvard University Press, 1950), 237–38.

Formula honestae vitae.
Instruction for the Honorable Life[1]

1. You seek something from me, my dearest brother, that I have never heard anyone to have sought from the one in whose care he is.* Nevertheless, because your devotion earnestly requests this, I am unable to say no to you, you who seek justly and reasonably something in the name of Christ: namely, that I depict in a brief sermon* the formula for the worthy‡ life. If you, afire with the love or affection of Christ, perseveringly observe this formula, you will without doubt obtain eternal life. Inasmuch as a word* proceeds from the interior man to the exterior, it is fitting that you unceasingly strive inwardly for the purity of your heart, where God, the lover of all purity, will deem it worthy to locate his seat, just as God locates a seat for himself in heaven. As Scripture states, *heaven is a seat for me,** and, *The soul of the just man is the seat of wisdom.** It is necessary, therefore, that you vigilantly always direct your thoughts to the good and the worthy,* so that you fear to think or meditate before God what you would deservedly blush to say or do before other people.

a suo provisore

*sermo
‡*honestae*

*sermo

*Isa 66:1
*Prov 12:23 LXX

*honestum

---

[1] *Honorable* here translates the Latin *honestae*, which is translated below according to context. This work is translated from PL 184:1167–72.

One knows that just as through our words or deeds we are made known to another person, so too we are surely made known through our thoughts to *the Spirit that searches all things,** because what words do for people, thoughts do for God. For God knows that the *thoughts of human beings are empty.** And just as no creature is invisible to God, absolutely nothing can be thought that is hidden from God. For the word* of God is alive and efficacious and is more penetrating than any double-edged sword, reaching all the way to the division of soul and spirit, to joint, too, and marrow, and *God is the discerner of the thoughts of the heart.**

2. Also, let Jesus always be in your heart, and let the image of the crucified one never depart from your mind. Let him be *your food and drink,** your sweetness and comfort, your honey and your desire, your reading and your meditation, your prayer and contemplation, your life, death, and resurrection. Always think about him, now placed in the manger* and wrapped up with swaddling clothes,* now presented to his Father in the temple by his parents,* now fleeing into Egypt,* staying there a long time in extreme poverty and need, and returning from there with the greatest hardship.* Now in the temple, listening to and questioning the teachers,* he who teaches knowledge to humankind,* and afterward, subject to his parents,* he to whom every creature is subject by law,‡ then hungry and thirsting in the desert,# he who is the bread of life≈ and the fountain of wisdom◊ and who *pastures amongst the lilies*† and fills every creature with blessing.∞

Now, weary from the trip, he sits thus above the well, talking alone with only the woman,* appointed ruler of the whole world; afterward, made into a victim for sacrifice, stretched out beyond limit, praying, and guiding all things sufficiently for all people.* And likewise, reflect on him himself, who is the sweetness

*1 Cor 2:10

*Ps 94:11

*sermo

*Heb 4:12

*John 6:35, 48, 51-59

*Luke 2:7, 16
*Luke 2:7
*Luke 2:22-39
*Matt 2:13

*Matt 2:21
*Luke 2:46
*Ps 94:10
*Luke 2:51
‡Heb 2:10
#Matt 4:2
≈John 6:35, 48
◊Sir 1:5
†Song 2:16
∞Ps 144:16

*John 4:6-26

*1 Cor 9:22

and consolation of angels and of human beings, nonetheless receiving consolation from an angel;* reflect on that One who is the support of the whole world bound and lashed against a column.‡ He himself who is the splendor of the angels, smeared[2] with spittle,# slapped in the face,° crowned with thorns,◊ drenched in disgrace.†

Finally, reflect on him condemned along with the iniquitous,∞ hanging in your place on the cross and dying, and commending his spirit to the hands of the Father.≈ Surely in this way your beloved will be a bundle of myrrh;Δ thus will he abide[3] between your breasts.⊚ In this way, gather together just this kind of bundle from all the cares and sorrows of your Lord, so that you prepare for yourself the bitter cup of tears. But if when you have been kindled by the most ardent love of Christ you should now wish along with the apostle to come to know that one, and not according to the flesh,* you will lift up the eyes of your mind a little[4] to the victory of the resurrected one, to the glory of the one ascending to the glorious majesty, seated and reigning in the glory of God the Father, savoring the things that are above and seeking the things which are above, where Christ sits at the right hand of God.* Nevertheless, do not long delay there, lest perhaps, if you should be a scrutinizer of the majesty for rather too long a time, you be obliterated by glory.*

*Luke 22:43
‡Matt 27:26;
Mark 15:15;
John 19:1
#Matt 27:30;
Mark 15:19
°lit. "struck by palms in the face";
Matt 27:30; Mark 15:19; John 19:3
◊Matt 27:29;
Mark 15:17;
John 19:2
†Matt 27:27-30;
Mark 15:16-20;
John 19:1-3
∞Matt 27:38;
Mark 15:27-29;
Luke 23:33
≈Luke 23:46
ΔJohn 19:39
⊚Song 1:13
*2 Cor 5:16

*Col 3:1-2

*Prov 25:27

[2] *Illitum* may also mean "anointed," providing a rich double meaning already implicit in the mystery of the Gospel event.

[3] The author varies verbs throughout the passage but here tellingly repeats *commoror*, a verb used earlier in the paragraph to describe the child Christ's time in Egypt. This repetition seems to liken the Lord's flight into Egypt and dwelling there "in extreme poverty" to his descent into the human heart.

[4] Perhaps an implicit reference to Ps 131:1: "O LORD, my heart is not lifted up, my eyes are not raised too high; I do not occupy myself with things too great and too marvelous for me."

3. Soberly and above all know that you ought to flee every exaltation, boastfulness, and arrogance of the heart as from vipers, knowing without a doubt that all those who praise their own heart before God are unclean. And thus you should scorn no one, harm no one, drag no one down, but out of love for Christ seek to serve everyone. But you should not only believe from the inmost desire of your heart that you are so inferior and so much more vile than others, but should not even say that you have progressed; nor should you consider yourself to be anything, just as the apostle says: *Whoever considers himself to be anything* *Gal 6:3   *when he is nothing deceives himself.**

4. Further, let your stride be full of maturity, weighty *honestus*   and respectable:* namely, you should walk neither with breaking steps[5] nor by turning the shoulders to the right and to the left, nor by lifting your neck or puffing out your chest, nor even by inclining your head above your shoulder, all of which either reek with levity, exhibit pride, or smack of hypocrisy. Therefore, when you are walking, standing, or sitting, *animo*   always have your face down, repeating in your mind* *Gen 3:19   that *you are dust and to dust you shall return,** and always have your heart above, where *Christ is sitting at* *Col 3:2-4   *the right hand of God the Father.** In whatever direction you look, you should look rather from necessity than from curiosity. But when you are sad, especially in community, it is fitting to conceal your sadness, presenting some kind of cheerfulness in your face: in private, however, your face should never be changed

---

[5] Aristotle describes the slow stride of the magnanimous man in *Nicomachean Ethics* 4.3. See Thomas Aquinas, *Summa Theologiae* II–II, q. 129, a. 3, ad. 3. See also Craig Steven Titus, *Resilience and the Virtue of Fortitude: Aquinas in Dialogue with the Pyschosocial Sciences* (Washington, DC: The Catholic University Press, 2006), 193–94, for an account of Aquinas's appropriation of this trait of the magnanimous man.

to a contrary expression. If in the presence of others you are moved to laughter for some reason, may your laughter not be shaking, as is wont to happen. For as Wisdom says, *your bodily clothing and the laughter of the teeth* (may your wit be without bite) *and the gait of a man makes that one known.** (*Likewise, intersperse joy amidst your cares from time to time.*)[6]

5. Never be idle; rather, read or mediate on something from the Holy Scriptures, or indeed, what is better, ruminate on the Psalms; nevertheless, ruminate while doing unceasingly what you have been commanded, so that the devil may always find you busy: *for idleness teaches many vices.*[7]* Read gladly those scriptures that especially inflame your mind more toward Christ. *Understand what I say: for the Lord will give you understanding in all things** if, in your mind, you have reflected upon the providence of God. When you pray, do not fill the ears of those who hear with sobs and deep sighs, but watchfully pray to God in the inner

*Sir 19:30

*Eccl 33:29

*2 Tim 2:7

---

[6] The two texts in parentheses do not appear in the Vulgate (either the Clementine or the Weber/Gryson edition) as part of the cited verse from Sirach, although at least the first seems to be presented as a scriptural quotation in Ps-Bernard's text; according to VulSearch, neither appears elsewhere in the Clementine edition of the Vulgate. The first (*sales tui sint sine dente*) is not included in the text of the *Formula honestae vitae* as it is printed in the *Opera* of Bernard of Clairvaux (Basil, 1566), 1256a. However, notes in later editions indicate that the verse has sometimes been included in the text (Sancti Bernardi, *Opera Omnia*, ed. Joannis Mabillon, editio quarta, emendata et aucta, 2 vols [Paris, 1839], 2:1584A). J.-P. Migne (PL 184:1169C) lists it as an alternate text in brackets within the body of the text. The second passge (*Tuis etiam interdum interpone gaudia curis*) appears without controversy in the text of all editions cited above. It seems to be a paraphrase from the *Catonis Disticha*, a collection of proverbs and moralisms attributed to a Dionysius Cato (distinct from the Roman poet of similar name) and used in Latin instruction from the 4th to the 18th centuries (*Cato Dist*, Lib 12).

[7] See RB 17–19, on praying the Psalms.

chamber of your heart.[8] Yet in order to obtain devotion and compunction it will be profitable if you are thus in solitude so that, raising pure hands to God, you can hear his voice. Watch your intention rising to heaven always, so that your heart may be where *Christ is, sitting at the right hand of God.** From praying, return again to reading, and again, having read, when loathing stirs return to praying.

*Col 3:1-2

6. Avoid the fellowship of the young, and especially of those who are beardless, as much as you are able to according to fittingness. Never fix your eyes into the face of anyone.

7. Approach your food as though you were approaching the cross: that is, never feed yourself according to pleasure, but only according to necessity, and let hunger, not taste, prompt your appetite.[9] Flee singularity, and be content with community, knowing that the body must be fed and that vices must be extinguished. Whenever something is placed before you, accept it as if administered by God, still having this always in mind and will, that the plate could be placed before another.[10]

8. Put a limit to your foresight in order that you do not seem wise to yourself. Always and everywhere

---

[8] Reverence at prayer is discussed in the Rule of Saint Benedict: "In the community, however, prayer should always be brief; and when the superior gives the signal, all should rise together" (RB 20.5; *RB 1980: The Rule of St. Benedict in Latin and English with Notes*, ed. Timothy Fry [Collegeville, MN: Liturgical Press, 1981], 216–17) (hereafter Fry).

[9] This matter is discussed in the Rule of Saint Benedict in the discussion on the measure of food and drink (RB 39–40; Fry 238–41). The Rule discusses receiving all things according to necessity, citing Acts 4:35: "distribution was made to each one as he had need" (RB 34.1; Fry 230–31).

[10] The Rule expresses this same sentiment: "they carry out the superior's order as promptly as if the command came from God himself" (RB 5.4; Fry 186–87).

and in all works have fear in order that you not haphazardly overstep a boundary in anything. Hence the blessed Job says, *I feared all my works, knowing that you did not spare the offender.* *   *Job 9:28

9. When you arrive weary at your bed, position yourself by lying most chastely;* do not lie on your   *honestissime
back or cross your legs.[11] For if perhaps the pomp of luxury should agitate you, call to mind your Beloved,[12] *lying in a bed of sorrows, and in his sickness his whole couch is overturned,* saying this in your heart, "My Lord   *Ps 41:3
hangs on a gibbet, and will I give myself to pleasure?"[13] And thus, once you have invoked the name of the Savior, when you many times repeat the name of salvation, the disturbance will finally cease, by the help of God. Let sleep overtake you as you are ruminating on the Psalms so that in sleep you may dream that you are praying the Psalms.

10. When you rise for vigils, praise your Creator with all your might, and lift up your voice with strength to the praise of your Redeemer. Finally, always have the purest love toward Christ, and remember to love anything other than him only for his sake. I have described for you, with more prolixity than I had planned, what I myself am unable to do, desiring that that which I know to be lacking in me be fulfilled in you, because your progress is my joy and crown in the Lord.*   *Phil 4:1;
1 Thess 2:19

---

[11] Lit. "do not join your heels to your shinbones by raising your knees."

[12] The word *pompa* literally refers to a procession or an array. The renunciation of Satan in the Latin baptismal rite contains a renunciation of "Satan with all his pomps [*omnibus pompis eius*]." See A. A. R. Toon Bastiaensen, "Exorcism: Tackling the Devil by Word of Mouth," in *Demons and the Devil in Ancient and Medieval Christianity*, ed. Nienke Vos and Willemien Otten (Leiden and Boston: Brill, 2011), 141.

[13] Alluding to Sarah's words in Gen 18:12.

A Useful Admonition about the Consideration of Death

Whenever you are struck with tedium, place yourself in meditation next to the stone upon which the dead bodies are washed and carefully think on the way these bodies are handled when buried: sometimes they are turned on their back, sometimes on their face. Think how the head nods, the arms fall to the side, the legs are stiff, the shinbones lie down; consider how they are clothed, sown together, and laid down when buried. Think how they are placed together in the tomb, how they are covered with dust, how they are devoured by worms, how they are consumed as if a rotten sack. Let the assiduous meditation on death be for you the highest philosophy. Carry it* with you no matter where you are and wherever you go, and you shall not sin into eternity.

*death

Brief and Highly Useful Admonition

In all your thoughts, words, and actions, say to yourself, "Would you act in this manner if you knew without any doubt that this was the very last hour of your life?" Pay attention to yourself, servant of God, lest you appear to condemn those whom you do not wish to imitate. It is uncertain in what place death expects you, so expect it in all places. Know yourself, and watch over the time that the mercy of the Creator has granted you to repent and to merit eternal glory. Be a cheerful giver, a rare demander, a modest receiver. Let your speech, in the time you have been given, be either serious or be none at all; let your appearance be either attentive or downcast or inwardly restrained: *May your eye be in your head.** Let your laughter either reveal or provoke mildness of spirit, but let it be rare. And let it out sometimes, but never

*Sir 2:14

guffaw.[14] Moreover, be so modest that you may not be held suspect of levity of spirit. Be kind to all, flattering to no one, familiar to few, fair to all. May God grant us all these things. Amen.

[14] The Rule discusses laughter in the context of silence and humility: "But coarse jests, and idle words or speech provoking laughter, we condemn everywhere to eternal exclusion; and for such speech we do not permit the disciple to open his lips" (RB 6.8; Fry 190–91). The tenth and eleventh degrees of humility: "The tenth degree of humility is that he is not given to ready laughter, for it is written: *Only a fool raises his voice in laughter* (Sir 21:23). The eleventh degree of humility is that a monk speaks gently and without laughter, seriously and with becoming modesty, briefly and reasonably, but without raising his voice, as it is written: 'A wise man is known by his few words'" (RB 7.59–61; Fry 200–201).

Instructio sacerdotalis.
Instruction for a Priest: A Treatise on the Principal Mysteries of Our Religion[1]

Preface

From brother Bernard, that servant old and new, to a reverend priest—walk in newness of life!*[2] It is sufficiently and abundantly clear how, with panting desire and burning intention, your heart warms you from within, how in your meditation it glows with fire, blazing in your bones.[3]* When I was in your presence you enjoined upon me this task, and when I was absent you wrote to me; urging me on once again, you commanded by means of a faithful messenger that I should collect some sparks for you,

*Rom 6:4

*Jer 20:9

---

[1] This treatise is translated from PL 184:771–92.

[2] Bernard of Clairvaux incorporates this Pauline phrase into several of his sermons, including Circ 3.5 (SBOp 4:286; CF 51:147), and Pasc 1:18 (SBOp 5:94; CF 52:148), as well as his *De consideratione* (Csi) 5.10.23 (SBOp 3:486; CF 37:168).

[3] Ps-Bernard is combining imagery common to monastic writings of his day. See Rupert Deutz's use of *anhelanti desiderio* in *De sancta trinitate et operibus eius* (CCCM 23; PL 167:867A), and Guibert of Nogent's use of *æstuabat intentio* in his *Epistula Guiberti ad Lysiardum Suessionensem episcopum* (PL 156:680B; CCCM 66–66A).

sparks flying out of that great furnace of charity[4]—the
Word incarnate.[5] But who am I that I should presume

*Ps 73:9
to set my mouth against the heavens?* For it is written,
*Exod 19:12-13
The beast which touches the mountain shall be stoned,[6]*
*Sir 3:22
and again, *Seek not for yourself higher things,** and, *The*
*Prov 25:27
one who scrutinizes majesty will be overwhelmed by glory.*
I am hemmed in, then, on two fronts: what you demand lies beyond my strength, yet I fear to deny you
what you ask. For I know the one who said, "Let a
good work be in your will for us: for with divine assistance it will come to perfection," and "the strength
that ignorance withholds, charity doles out."[7]

Accept therefore some lines from Sacred Scripture,
taken from here and there, and if, with the palate of
your pious heart, you sense in these anything fragrant,

---

[4] A variant reading is *claritatis*, indicating clarity or splendor,
instead of the *charitatis* of the PL.

[5] See Peter Cellensis's use of the image of the *caminus chari-
tatis* in *Sermo XI: in nativitate Domini IV* (PL 202:669C) and
Guibert of Nogent's in *Epistularium Guiberti: Epistulae Guiberti,*
Ep 46.36 (CCCM 66–66A). For a critical study on Guibert of
Nogent's influence on monastic writers of his day, see Jay
Rubenstein, *Guibert of Nogent: Portrait of a Medieval Mind* (New
York: Routledge, 2002).

[6] In his edition Migne includes a reference to Heb 12:10 (PL
184:773A) that we have omitted.

[7] This section quotes and reworks part of Homily 21.1 from
Gregory the Great's *XL Homiliarum in Evangelia* (CCSL 141:174):
"the strength that ignorance withholds, charity doles out [*uires
quas imperitia denegat caritas ministrat*]. For I know the one who
said: 'Open your mouth, and I will fill it' [Ps 81:10] [*Scio namque
qui dixit: 'Aperi os tuum et ego adimplebo illud'*]. Let a good work
be in your will for us: for with divine assistance it will come to
perfection [*Bonum ergo opus nobis in uoluntate sit, nam ex diuino
adjutorio erit in perfectione*]" (Gregory the Great, *Forty Gospel
Homilies,* trans. Dom David Hurst, CS 123 [Kalamazoo, MI:
Cistercian Publications, 1990], 157–58 [hereafter Hurst, trans.,
Homilies]). Gregory uses the line *Scio enim qui dixit* to refer to
God's speech in Psalm 81. Ps-Bernard changes the referent of
"I know the one who said" to Gregory.

anything sweet—some interior flavor—do not attribute it to me; rather, give glory to those noble sellers of unguents from whose storehouses[8] they have been obtained.[9] Your intention, unless I am mistaken, was for it to be explained to you, by genuine authorities and suitable examples, in what way Christ, although on the altar he is hidden and veiled beneath the species of bread, nevertheless remains in the splendor of infinite and inestimable clarity.[10] You ought to know that to understand this is not for the pilgrim* but for one who comprehends,* not for the exile in the valley of weeping* but for the citizen of the heavenly homeland, not for the one fighting but for the one triumphant.* This is not given to those running but to those having arrived.* It does not precede merit but is added to the reward.

*Jer 14:8
*Phil 3:12
*Ps 83:7
*2 Tim 4:7
*1 Cor 9:24

Who then is greater or equal to that one who, after the rapture and preeminence of the third heaven, and after mysterious heavenly things were observed of which *it is not permitted for man to speak,** said, *We see now through a mirror in an enigma, then, however, face to face*, and again, *Now I know in part; then I will know as also I am known?** Who would presume to see himself as a vessel of election* if the eye of conscience within has been darkened?* In the meantime, let us nevertheless see with that one, through a mirror and in an enigma, what we are able, and if we are not yet able

*2 Cor 12:2-4
*1 Cor 13:12
*Acts 9:15
*Matt 6:22-23

---

[8] See Bernard of Clairvaux, SC 23.7 (SBOp 1:138–50; CF 7:31).

[9] Compare Ps-Bernard's reticence to speak of divine matters with that of Bernard of Clairvaux in his *Liber de gradibus humilitatis et superbiæ* (Hum) Praef (SBOp 3:16; CF 13:28); and *Liber de diligendo Deo* Prol (Dil) (SBOp 3:119; CF 13:93).

[10] This is the first appearance of *claritas*, a term that later is more technically used in the *Pars Secunda* in reference to the splendor of Christ's body in the Transfiguration and the Eucharist. For this reason, we normally translate it as *clarity* except when otherwise noted.

*2 Cor 3:18

to see the glory of the Lord with unveiled face* (as we are also not able to look directly upon the chariot of the sun), let us, with a cloud interposed between us, strive at least to be illuminated to a certain degree by his rays.*

*Mark 9:2-8

According to what has been set forth about this plan, with the grace of God leading the way, let us accomplish what we can. Therefore, before we say a few things, we are dividing the series of things to be said into only three parts,[11] noting beforehand three gifts that the Wisdom of God has preordained from eternity to be brought together for us, or, rather, one gift with three operations, to be brought together for three purposes. First, that the Son of God, dying for us, gave himself to us; second, that he gives himself to us in the Eucharist; third, that he gives himself to us in eternal life.

PART ONE:
That the Son of God Gave Himself for us in Dying for us

Chapter One:
Concerning the Fall of Humankind from the Dignity of the Primeval Condition

1. *Every best and perfect gift comes from above, descending from the Father of lights, in the presence of whom there is no change nor shadow of vicissitude.** The gift is best because the Giver is best. For as Boethius said, *He is the best and highest maker, and from him all hatefulness is*

*Jas 1:17

---

[11] The Latin here reads *capitulas*, but it is translated as *parts* because of Ps-Bernard's consistent use of that term. In light of the Christological nature of the text, an alternative translation could be *heads*, since each part is defined in reference to Christ, the Head of the church.

greatly removed.[12] See, O human, what he himself paid for you, and even more what he paid in advance, and paid over and above.[13] He created you when you did not exist, and he recreated you when you were lost; he created you so that you would be a participant in his blessedness, and he recreated you so that after the Fall you might not be permanently deprived of your homeland and eternal happiness. He created you *to his image and similitude,** conferring what is natural to the image and imparting grace to the similitude,[14] so that you might excel in the mind and defeat all irrationalities with reason. *And other living things are bent so that they see the earth, but he gave a lofty countenance*

*Gen 1:26

[12] The source of this passage is unknown, but Boethius describes God the Creator and the created world made in the divine image (*similique in imagine*) in his poem "O qui perpetua" (*De Consolatione Philosophiae* 3.9). Anonymous of Einsiedeln (9th–11th century), in his commentary on Boethius's "O qui perpetua," refers to a close parallel to the second clause of this passage that occurs in Plato's *Timaeus*, which reads, *Optimus erat, ab optimo porro inuidia longe relegata est* (Anonymous of Einsiedeln; CCCM 171:117; *Timaeus: Plato secundum translationem quam fecit Chalcidius*, PL 578A:22). Peter Abelard (d. 1142) also quotes this line from Plato in his *Theologia Christiana* (CCCM 12:361). Finally, a similar passage can be found in John of Salisbury's (d. 1180) *Policraticus* 2.12: *Optimus est, inquit, porro ab optimo longe relegata est omnis invidia* (CCCM 118:91). Thus although the author whom Ps-Bernard used here is uncertain, it is possible that he was using the commentary of Anonymous of Einsiedeln, as it is apparently the only text that explains both the quotation from Plato and its attribution to Boethius.

[13] This is the first of many instances where Ps-Bernard speaks of the price paid by God and by Christ. See, e.g., Part One, chap. 6, ¶7.

[14] The Latin reads *ad imaginem conferens tibi naturalia; ad similitudinem largiens gratuita.* Ps-Bernard's interpretation of the natural things (*naturalia*) that come from the divine image and the supernatural things (*gratuita*) that come from the similitude becomes more evident throughout this paragraph. See n. 11.

to humans, and he commanded them to look to the sky and, standing up, to raise their faces to the stars.[15] So being always mindful of what is above, may you keep your Creator in mind and ceaselessly remind your soul of its origin. For God made you, as was stated above, to his image and similitude: to his image in order that you might have memory, intellect, discretion, and other natural things; to his similitude in order that you might have innocence, justice, and other graces: to his image, in the knowledge of truth; to his similitude, in the love of virtue. Certainly, you have been made to the image of God, since all these things have been brought together for you, and you have been made to his similitude according to the essence of the deity, immortal and indivisible.[16] Every creature was made

---

[15] P. Ovidii Nasonis, *Metamorphoses* 1.84–86 (*Metamorphoses, Books 1–8*, ed. Jeffrey Henderson, Loeb Classical Library no. 42 [Cambridge, MA: Harvard University Press, 1984]). This passage from Ovid is also used by the Venerable Bede, *In principium Genesis usque ad nativitatem Isaac* 1.1.26 (CCSL 118A:26), and by Alexander of Hales, *Summa theologica* 1.2.1 (Florence: College of St. Bonaventure, 1930).

[16] In the preceding section, Ps-Bernard offers his interpretation of the frequently cited Gen 1:26-27, on the creation of human beings according to the divine image and similitude. Augustine is one of the earliest and best-known authors to equate the image with reason, memory, and will, present throughout his *Confessiones* (see especially book 10, on memory; CCSL 27:155–93). It is also a common subject in medieval monastic works, including those of Bernard of Clairvaux. His Dil 2.2–3 speaks of the "dignity" (*dignitatis*), knowledge, and virtue in the human soul (SBOp 3:121–22; CF 13:95–96). It is also a common theme in his *Sermones super Cantica Canticorum*, where he distinguishes the image from the rational soul, again refers to its "dignity" (SC 24.5–7 [SBOp 1:156–59; CF 7:46–47]), and further describes the image as the source of justice, wisdom, and truth, in a similar fashion to Ps-Bernard (SC 80.2–5 [SBOp 2:277–81; CF 40:146–50]). See also Aelred of Rievaulx, *De Anima* (CCCM 1:683–754; CF 22). For studies of the medieval significance of the theme, see Robert Javelet, *Image et ressemblance au XIIe siècle, de saint Anselme à Alain de Lille*, 2 vols. (Paris: Éditions Letouzey

because of you: heaven, in order that you might have a homeland and delight in its beautiful appearance, and the land, in order that it might bear the most delightful and beautiful fruit for you. He made the sun and the moon and the other stars to shine[17] for you; he gave you dominion over the flying creatures of heaven and the beasts of the field and the fish of the sea in order that you might have dominion over all these things for your pleasure.* Behold *the best and perfect gift that has been given, descending from above.**[18] What more ought he to have done for you that he did not do?*

    2. Yet after these great and numerous gifts you transgressed, so that you passed into a most evil place: from life to death, from incorruption to corruption, from freedom to servitude, from glory to punishment, from innocence to guilt, from your homeland into exile, from joy to sorrow, from beatitude to misery, from rest to toil. And though you were a member of the celestial citizens, you have become subjugated to demons,[19] and though you were able by the revealed form constantly and fully to enjoy the desirable sight

*Gen 1:26

*Jas 1:17

*see Isa 5:4

& Ané, 1967); David N. Bell, *The Image and Likeness: The Augustinian Spirituality of William of Saint Thierry*, CS 78 (Kalamazoo, MI: Cistercian Publications, 1984); Luke Anderson, *The Image and Likeness of God in Bernard of Clairvaux's Free Choice and Grace* (Bloomington: AuthorHouse, 2005).

[17] Literally, "shining." That is, *lucentia* is an adjectival predicative of the object *solem et lunam, et caetera sidera*.

[18] Ps-Bernard returns to the verse from James with which he began the chapter and quotes it in a condensed form: *Ecce datum optimum et donum perfectum desursum descendens*.

[19] *Subjugalis*, here translated as *subjugated*, is found in Matt 21:5. It is often translated as "beast of burden" or "accustomed to the yoke." Thus this sentence might read literally, "you have become accustomed to the yoke of demons." Given that this paragraph later contains references to Luke 10, Ps-Bernard may also be drawing a parallel to Luke 10:17, in which the seventy-two disciples sent by Jesus rejoice that the demons have been made subject to them (*daemonia subiciuntur nobis*).

*claritatis

*1 Pet 1:12

*Lam 4:5

*Ps 83:7

*Luke 10:30-37

of the divine splendor,* into which *the angels desire to look,** thereafter you were forced to see your disgrace and your shame, and according to the prophet, *you who were brought up in saffron embraced dungheaps.*[20]*
Having been exiled from the place of bliss, from the Paradise of delightfulness, you were finally thrust down into the valley of tears;* you became that miserable traveler, or rather that deviator, who went down from Jerusalem to Jericho and fell into the hands of mercenaries, into the judgment of malicious spirits who, having wounded him in natural things, stripped him of graces as well and left him half-dead and forsaken, afflicted by a double death of body and soul.[21]*
And this is the time of your straying. For the diligence of the learned distinguishes four times for the human race, according to four conditions: the time of straying, the time of recalling, the time of reconciliation, and the time of pilgrimage.[22]

[20] The quotation from Lamentations has some slight differences from the Vulgate, which reads *qui nutriebantur in croceis amplexati sunt stercora.*

[21] Throughout his opening paragraphs, Ps-Bernard greatly emphasizes the duality of body and soul, or of natural things (*naturalia*) and graces (*gratuita*). So in the first paragraph, he speaks of what is natural according to the image and of graces according to similitude; here in the second paragraph he uses the analogy of the unfortunate traveler to illustrate the loss of both. Aquinas employs Luke 10:30 in the same way in the ST I–II.85.1 *sed contra,* which comes from the *Glossa Ordinaria* of Strabo (though Aquinas cites the Venerable Bede).

[22] These four "times"—*deviationis, revocationis, reconciliationis,* and *peregrinationis*—are also employed by several other medieval liturgists and theologians. One of the earliest to discuss the times at length is John Beleth (d. 1182). He delineates the duration of each in his *Summa de Ecclesiasticis Officiis* 55 (CCCM 41A:97–98). He also draws numerous analogies of the four times, likening them to the four seasons of the solar year, the nativity, passion, resurrection, and visitation of Christ, and the state of human beings before and after baptism, among other instances. A similar discussion is found in noted liturgist and

Chapter Two:
On the Time of Straying

3. The time of straying reached from the fall of the first human beings to the time of Abraham, who accepted the commandment of circumcision as a sign of faith* and was the first to hear from the Lord the promise of grace, when the Lord said to him, *All the nations will be blessed through your seed.** Thence the apostle Paul says, *The promises were made to Abraham, and to his seed. He did not say "To your seeds," referring to many; but referring to one, "And to your seed, who is Christ."** And Luke the herald or, better, the evangelist of the same grace, says about the incarnation of the Word, *The oath that the Lord swore to Abraham our father, that he would give himself to us.** It is called the time of straying, because however many lived in this time, nearly all turned away from the path of truth. *They did not call upon God,* and *the fear of God was not before their*

*Rom 4:11

*Gen 22:18

*Gal 3:16

*Luke 1:73

---

canonist Sicard of Cremona's (d. 1215) *Mitralis de officiis* (CCCM 228:292–93). Sicard quotes Beleth directly and also explains the four times in an explicitly liturgical way, corresponding them to the night, dawn, midday, and evening prayers (*nocti, mane, meridiei,* and *vespere*) as well as to the periods of time between Septuagesima, the eighth Sunday of Easter, the eighth Sunday of Pentecost, and Advent. Two later authors for whom the four times feature prominently are William Durand (d. 1296) and Jacob of Voragine (d. 1298). In Durand's *Rationale divinorum officiorum* 6.1.2–5 (CCCM 140A:120–22), the times are described according to the annual seasons (both solar and liturgical) and also in terms of "light" and "obscurity"; that is, humanity is subject to great ignorance and obscurity in the time of straying (*deviationis*) but gains "much light" by the time of pilgrimage (*peregrinationis*). Finally, Jacob of Voragine's famed *Golden Legend* delineates the same four times according to the liturgical models mentioned above (*Legenda aurea [vulgo Historia lombardica dicta]*, ed. Johann Grässe [Osnabrück: Zeller, 1965], 1–2, 145–46, 235).

*Ps 13:3-5

eyes,[23]* although there were a few exceptions: namely Enoch, who was snatched up lest evil turn his understanding away from God, and Noah, who was saved in the ark with eight other souls so that he would not *Sir 44:16-17*   be swallowed in the flood.[24]*

Chapter Three:
On the Time of Recalling

4. The time of recalling stretched from Abraham until the coming of the Redeemer, and it was in this time that the Trinitarian faith first began to bloom. Already with the patriarchs it flowered, with the kings it brought forth fruit, and with the prophets its fruit *Luke 1:78*   ripened, for the *Dayspring from on high has visited us.** And rightly is this time called the time of recalling, *for the God and Father of our Lord Jesus Christ, the Father of* *2 Cor 1:3*   *mercies and the God of all consolation,** had already at this time considered the human race with *thoughts of* *Jer 29:11*   *peace and not of affliction.** He arranged to call back the *Luke 15:1-7*   sheep that had been lost,* he sent patriarchs, he gave the Law, he advised by means of signs and marvels, he offered innumerable helps;[25] finally, *because of the*

---

[23] Ps-Bernard quotes the beginning of Ps 13:5 (*Deum non invocaverunt*) and the end of Ps 13:3 (*non erat timor Dei ante oculos eorum*), with minor changes from the Vulgate (*Deum* rather than *Dominus*, and *erat* rather than *est*).

[24] Ps-Bernard again takes up this reference in Part One, chap. four, referring what Sir 44:17 says about Noah (*et in tempore iracundiae factus est reconciliatio*) to Christ.

[25] Ps-Bernard's description of the time of recalling is clearly biblically based, but he may also have been familiar with Isidore of Seville's "Homily on the Feast of the Lord's Birth," found in *De ecclesiasticis officiis* 1.26.1: *Volens ergo Deus terminare peccatum, consuluit verbo, lege, prophetis, signis, plagis, prodigiis. Sed cum nec sic quidem errores suos ammonitus agnosceret mundus, misit deus filium suum ut carne indueretur, et hominibus appareret, et peccatores sanaret* (CCSL 113:29).

abundant love with which He loved us,* *he sent his only-*   *Eph 2:4
begotten Son in the likeness of flesh, yet without sin,* *so*   *Rom 8:3
that he might cleanse all, and this time is truly *the time*
for showing mercy* and *the year of kindness.‡*   *Ps 101:14
                                          ‡Ps 64:12

Chapter Four:
On the Time of Reconciliation

5. The time of reconciliation began from this time
and lasted until the mystery of our redemption was
accomplished, when that saving victim who was
sacrificed reconciled us to God the Father; of him it is
truly written, *Behold the great priest, who in his days*
pleased God and has been found just,[26] and *in the time of*
wrath he made reconciliation:* *no one like him has been*   *Sir 44:17
found.* About this reconciliation the apostle Paul says,   *Sir 44:20
We are ambassadors for Christ; we beseech you, be recon-
ciled to God.* And truly this name *reconciliation* has   *2 Cor 5:20
arisen from what he accomplished.

Chapter Five:
On the Time of Pilgrimage

6. The time of pilgrimage is after the coming of the
Holy Spirit up to the end of the age, from which time
the faithful church began to recognize its condition of
pilgrimage and to long for its homeland. From this
place the vessel of election,* groaning, says, *As long as*   *Acts 9:15
we are in this world, we are wandering in a strange land

---

[26] The Latin text reads, *Ecce sacerdos magnus, qui in diebus suis*
placuit Deo, et inventus est justus. The antiphon *Ecce sacerdos*
magnus was in use as early as the 11th century for the feast of
the Chair of Peter (University of Waterloo, *CANTUS* database:
http://cantusdatabase.org/id/ 008040). It is listed in the *Car-*
mina Scripturarum: Ex Ecclesiastico 44:297, 21.

away from God,[27]* and David says, *Woe to me! For my tarrying here is prolonged!** Nevertheless, he consoles himself and says, *Worthy of my songs are your decrees, here in the place of my pilgrimage.** It is clear in these examples why this time is reckoned to be the time of pilgrimage.

*2 Cor 5:6
*Ps 119:5

*Ps 118:54

Chapter Six:
The Time of Reconciliation is Considered Further, and the Whole Work of the Redemption of Humankind is Explained Briefly

7. Having distinguished the four times along with the reasons for their names, consider, O human, the time of your redemption. Be mindful and remember how you have been redeemed. *You have been bought,* says the apostle Paul, *at a great price; glorify God and bear him in your body**—not only at a great price, but at the greatest price. You were *sold under sin** at a paltry and shameful price with the bite of one fruit; you have been bought and redeemed at a great and inestimable price by the death of the Son of God. What is more costly than this price? What is more inestimable? He through whom all things were made and *without whom nothing was made,** the only-begotten Son of the Father Most High, consubstantial and coeternal with the same Father, equal in majesty and glory, identical in essence, *the power and wisdom of God:** this one of such kind and such greatness, *although he was in the form of God, he emptied himself, taking on the form of a slave;** he descended from the bosom of the Father into our *valley*

*1 Cor 6:20
*Rom 7:14

*John 1:3

*1 Cor 1:24

*Phil 2:6-7

---

[27] Here Ps-Bernard seems to be paraphrasing 2 Cor 5:1-6, which speaks of the groaning of those who are far from heaven and absent from the Lord.

*of tears;** he made himself small[28] in the womb of a   *Ps 83:7
virgin, and he who was in the beginning with God
was made the abbreviated Word.[29]*   *John 1:1-3, 14
And see how abbreviated—that boundless one—
how small he was made! He enclosed himself within
the insides of a girl. There, having been surrounded
with bloody bindings, he bore the tediousness of nine
months. Then he was brought forth into the light, and
he cried, as a baby cries. He was enfolded within filthy
rags according to our wretched custom, and, bound
with swaddling bands, he was laid in a manger near
the breathing of dumb animals and placed in a stink-
ing stable next to his impoverished mother.

What letter teaches, what tongue speaks, what im-
ages show that anyone of those born in the human
race has labored with the burden of such poverty? The
nourisher of all was nourished with human milk; he
was filthy in his rags in order that you might not be
filthy in your sins. He was circumcised in the flesh in   ‡see Deut 10:16;
30:6; Jer 4:4; 9:25-
order that you might be circumcised in mind.‡ He   26; Rom 2:29;
Col 2:11
humbled himself to be baptized under the hands of
his own servant John in the Jordan,* not in order to   *Matt 3:13-17;
Mark 1:9-11;
wash off any stain from him who entered the world   Luke 3:21-22

---

[28] The verb here, *contraxit*, is difficult to render into English.
Translated literally, the sentence would read, "[Christ] con-
tracted himself into the womb of a virgin." The sense is that
Christ made himself small, diminished himself, or constricted
himself.

[29] The phrase *verbum abbreviatum*—"the abbreviated word"—
seems odd to the modern ear but was common in the Middle
Ages. The phrase is found in a number of Bernard of Clairvaux's
writings, including his *Sermones de nativitate domini* (Nat 1.1;
SBOp 4:244; CF 51:99) and Dil 7.21 (SBOp 3:136–37; CF 13:113),
referring to the "contraction" of the boundless Word into tem-
porality and human form. The phrase can be found in countless
other medieval texts, including Peter the Cantor's *Verbum
abbreviatum*, Bede's scriptural commentaries, John Cassian's
De incarnatione Christi contra Nestorium haereticum 6.6, and
Primasius Adrumetanensis's commentary on Romans.

*1 Pet 2:22

without stain and *who committed no sin, nor was guile found in his mouth*,* but in order to sanctify the waters for you, that the contact of his most pure flesh might confer regenerative power to the waters so that your crimes might be wiped away.

*Matt 4:1-11

8. Soon after being baptized, he set out into the desert* to offer you a model of sanctity and a pious way of life: there he fasted for forty days and forty nights, never in all that time tasting food; this is utterly impossible for human weakness, which, unless it has applied itself to restore the stomach's ruin with daily sustenance, will be subject to the injuries of deprivation. Therefore God became hungry willingly out of the necessity of his assumed nature, and withstood temptations from the devil: concerning the inordinate appetite for food he defeated the Tempter no less patiently than wisely and repelled his confusion. In this the Lord gathered three favors for you, O human: the model of humility, the form of patience, and the imitation of caution. If you are tempted, humble yourself, for *a slave is not greater than his master*.*

*John 15:20

*Job 7:1

The Lord was tempted, and his servant must also be tempted, for *the life of men on earth is a trial*.* However, since the temptations of the demons are manifold and subtle, the Lord warned Peter, saying, *Satan has demanded to sift you all like wheat*.* If you are tempted, suffer patiently. For although the Lord had the power and authority to cast the Tempter down to the lowest hell,[30] he bore temptation patiently and overcame it by means of reason. You must be cautious if you are tempted, lest the Tempter, transforming himself into an angel of light,* be able to deceive you under the appearance of righteousness, just like Eve, to whom

*Luke 22:31

*2 Cor 11:14

---

[30] A more literal translation might be, "Although the Lord could have cast the devil down to the lowest hell by his command" (*Dominus cum tentatorem suum imperio in ima inferni praecipitare potuisset*).

he said, *If you eat of the tree, you will be like gods, knowing good and evil.** Resist humbly, resist cautiously, resist patiently. *Gen 3:5

The Lord is faithful, says Scripture, *he will not allow you to be tempted beyond that which you are able to withstand; but with your temptation he will also provide a way forward, so that you should be able to withstand.** *The one who shall overcome,* it says, *I will make a pillar in my temple,** and again it says, *To the one who shall overcome, I will give him to eat of the tree of life, which is in the paradise of my God.** The sweet promise and the happy prize are for the one who has run well, and the blessed crown is for the one who has overcome well.* *1 Cor 10:13

*Rev 3:12

*Rev 2:7

*1 Cor 9:24-27; Gal 5:7-10; Phil 2:16; 3:13-14; 2 Tim 2:5; 4:8; Jas 1:12; Rev 2:10; 3:11

9. Therefore he was tempted, O human, not for himself but for you; for you he prevailed, not for himself; for you he hungered, for you he was thirsty and weary, because of you abuses and insults were heaped upon him, and on your account, he accepted all sufferings that were necessary and fitting[31] as his own. Except for sin, he excluded none of your weaknesses[32] from himself;* on your account, he has in various ways *worked salvation in the midst of the earth**—raising the dead, giving sight to the blind, restoring hearing to the deaf, steps to the lame, and cleanness to lepers, and performing countless other acts of power. He ran

*see Heb 4:15

*Ps 73:12

---

[31] In the medieval period, the notion of "fittingness," usually signified by the word *conveniens,* had to do with the most suitable means for achieving an end. In particular, the "fittingness" of the incarnation in bringing about the goal of human salvation was a recurring topic for reflection. Here the two verbs translated as *necessary* and *fitting* are *oportuit* and *decuit,* synonymous in force with *conveniens.* See Aquinas, ST III, q. 1, as well as Anselm of Canterbury, *Cur Deus Homo* 2.16 (*Pourquoi Dieu s'est fait homme,* ed. and trans. René Roques, SCh 91 [Paris: Éditions du Cerf, 2005]).

[32] On the human defects of body and soul that Christ co-assumed for the sake of human redemption, see Aquinas, ST III, q. 14, 15. See Peter Lombard, *Libri Quattor Sententiarum* 3 d.15.

*Luke 8:1

through cities and villages, he journeyed through streets and byways, preaching the Gospel with words and deeds* and demonstrating with signs and marvels the way of life.

That he might further show you examples of humility in himself, on the sixth day before he suffered[33] he desired to come to Jerusalem, humble upon a humble

*Matt 21:4-7;
see Zech 9:9

and lowly donkey,* and to be greeted by the crowds, that his every action might be your lesson and his whole life your education. He was handed over by the treacherous and damned Judas and sold for thirty

*Matt 26:15
*Rom 7:14

pieces of silver like a common slave,* so that you who have been *sold under sin** might receive redemption. Seated at supper with his blessed apostles the day before he suffered, he gave his flesh to eat and his

*John 6:52

blood to drink* and bequeathed to you the celebration of the same mystery in remembrance of him. Then, getting up from supper, girded with a linen cloth, he

*John 13:4-5

poured water into a basin.* And the King of Angels[34] humbled himself before the feet of his lowly servants: he did not disdain to touch, to clean, to wash with his

---

[33] Ps-Bernard's chronology of Christ's final days in Jerusalem appears to be a combination of the timelines presented in the Synoptics and John. While only John mentions the temporal detail of six days, the chronology presented here must assume that Jesus was crucified the day after Passover, as presented in the Synoptic accounts. If John's account were being closely followed, Jesus would actually enter Jerusalem on the fifth day before the feast of Passover (see John 12:12). Assuming a synthesis with the timeline of the Synoptics, Ps-Bernard's version has Jesus entering the city on the fifth day before Passover, but on the sixth day before his crucifixion.

[34] An ancient title for Christ (present in both Augustine and Cassiodorus) that appears in Bernard of Clairvaux's works occasionally. See *In festo Sancti Michaelis*, S 1.2: *quoque Creator et rex angelorum venit, non ministrari, sed ministrare, et animam suam dare pro multis* ["also the Creator and the King of Angels came not to be served, but to serve, and to give his own life for many"] (Matt 20:28) (SBOp 5:295; CF 54:92).

most pure hands the filthiness of their feet, filth that clung to them from dirt of the road. And he left you an example to do the same, saying, *If I have washed your feet, being your Lord and Master, so also ought you to wash each others' feet.** On what grounds, then, are you proud, *dirt and ash,** *filth and worm*‡ that you are? Why, rotten limb, do you exalt yourself above the Head who is feared by the angelic powers themselves?

10. Next the Lord was fixed in prayer, and on account of the anguish of his spirit* he was completely saturated with bloody sweat. There he was seized and held, and he was led before the seat of the judge; when many false testimonies went forth against him and they accused him with many lies, he was silent as an innocent lamb who was led as an offering.* *He did not open his mouth; as a man who does not hear, he did not have reproofs in his mouth.** There they spat upon the face of sweet Jesus, they struck him with blows, and the servants in turn slapped him on the head. From there he was bound to the pillar, and he was struck with whips, his flesh swelling because of the knots on the whips. His flesh turned black and blue, with blood running drop by drop from his wounds to the earth. Then with the pricking of the thorns they caused his head to bleed all over, and in mockery of him a rod was thrust into his hand and a scarlet mantle thrown about him, and he was laughed at as if he were a fool. I say but a little.

Here, O human, shudder all over, grow stiff with trembling, rightly grow pale, beat your breast with your fists, pour forth your whole soul with weeping, suffer with the one who suffered. He was led to death so that you might be led out of death: the impious instigators led him, they led the Lamb to be slain. They forced him to bear his own cross on his own shoulders and to carry it to the place of his passion. He did not protest, he did not murmur, he did not argue: he yielded to his torturers.

**John 13:14

**Sir 10:9

‡Job 25:6

**see Wis 5:3; Exod 6:9

**Isa 53:7

**Ps 37:14, 15

11. Consider this, O human, with what price, with what kind of price, and with how great a price you have been redeemed: you have not been redeemed with perishable things—with gold or with silver. A death without suffering[35] on the part of your Redeemer, Creator, and Fashioner did not suffice for you to be redeemed; see the manner of his death, consider the condition of his dying, and consider what you owe to the one who died. Behold how the just one died.* He was stretched out on the cross, his limbs were pulled apart, his back, still full of wounds from the fresh blows of the lashes and still dripping with fresh blood, was rubbed against the rough wooden bar of the cross. His hands and feet were pierced, the nails were struck into them with hammers, and the more deeply the nails penetrated, the more they tore apart the wounds (because of their thickness) and worsened his suffering. Gall mixed with vinegar was poured into his thirsty mouth, and wine mixed with myrrh was added.[36] The servants of the demon shook their heads, scoffing at the pain of the one hanging on the cross: *If he is the Son of God*, they said, *let him now come down from the cross, and we will believe in him,** as if they said, *so much dishonor and punishment binds him that he shall not rise again.**

12. Hereafter, most pious Redeemer, in order that you might revive my miserable soul from death, you delivered your most holy soul unto death by those most impious instigators, who were not satisfied until they pierced your side with the lance and collected the liquid of your blood when it overflowed—the blood by which we were redeemed. O soul, what can

*see Rom 5:7

*Matt 27:40, 42

*Ps 40:9;
Amos 5:1

---

[35] *Simplex mors*, lit. "a simple death," refers to a death without torture and humiliation, such as beheading, a form of execution reserved for Roman citizens.

[36] In the Vulgate, Matt 27:34 has "wine mixed with gall," Mark 15:23 has "wine mixed with myrrh," and Luke 23:36 and John 19:29 both have "vinegar."

you do? Who will provide the water for your head and the fountain of tears for your eyes, so that you might sufficiently lament and weep enough for this murder by your people? Your beloved is for you this *packet of myrrh,* * and not only a packet, but an immense burden of bitterness.[37] Suffer with the one suffering, that you may deserve to be redeemed. Be the dove in the hole of the rock, in the hollow of the wall.[38]* Fly into the hands, fly into the feet, swoop into the side so that you might leave nothing unsearched, and flood each member with the bitterness of compassion. Behold the price of your redemption, O ransomed one![39] Behold what manner of victim was sacrificed for your sin, for your transgression.

13. By what necessity* did he suffer those things, for what need* did he shed his blood so many times?[40] For it is said that he was sprinkled five times by the

*Song 1:12

*Song 2:14

*necessitate
*indigentia

[37] See Bernard of Clairvaux, SC 42.3, 42.7, and 43 (SBOp 2:34–35, 37, 41–44; CF 7:212, 215, 220–24), in which he speaks of the bitterness and the burden of the love of Christ.

[38] Vulg: *columba mea in foraminibus petrae in caverna maceriae ostende mihi faciem tuam sonet vox tua in auribus meis vox enim tua dulcis et facies tua decora.* On the dove in the cleft of the rock, see Bernard of Clairvaux, SC 61 and 62 (SBOp 2:148–61; CF 31: 140–60).

[39] The question of how Christ's passion brought about the salvation of the human race was a focal point of medieval Christological considerations. One popular explanation derived from certain letters of the New Testament (see 1 Pet 1:18 and Gal 3:13) was that the passion effected human salvation by way of redemption or ransom from bondage to sin. See Anselm of Canterbury, *Cur Deus Homo* 1.5 and Aquinas, ST III, q. 48, a. 4.

[40] The necessity or appropriateness of Christ's humiliation and suffering was a common theme in the work of medieval theologians. See Anselm of Canterbury, *Cur Deus Homo* 1.1: "with what necessity and reason God, although he is omnipotent, assumed the lowliness and weakness of human nature for our restoration" (*qua necessitate scilicet et ratione deus, cum sit omnipotens, humilitatem et infirmitatem humanae naturae pro eius restauratione assumpserit*). See also Aquinas, ST III, q. 46, aa. 1–4, 11.

shedding of his blood, which I have judged it not useless to describe with these verses:

> *Five times, and in five ways they wounded you, O Christ:*
> *circumcision, bloody sweat, scourging, crowning with*
> *thorns,*
> *and the five wounds of your side, hands, and feet.*[41]

He who was able to redeem humankind by the authority of the divine majesty alone endured such extraordinary things for the redemption of humanity. Listen,
O human—it was your need, not his own. The first
man[42] was united with the atoning action for his transgression, because he could not be purified without the
offering of a sacrifice. The mere human being was not
strong enough to offer a pure sacrifice,[43] because it was

[41] Through prophetic knowledge, Christ forsaw the sufferings
he was to undergo; his sweating of blood was thus caused by
his tormentors. Reflection upon the Five Wounds of Christ can
be found in several of Bernard of Clairvaux's works, including
SC 61.7–8 (SBOp 2:159–61; CF 31:146–47). A discussion of the
Five Wounds can be found in his first Sermon for Christmas
Day, Nat 1.8 (SBOp 4:250; CF 51:105–6). According to sacred
legend, Bernard asked Christ about his untold sufferings and
learned of the Sacred Wound of the Shoulder. He subsequently
composed a prayer in devotion to this wound.

[42] The word translated here as *first man* is *protoplastus*, trans-
literated from the Greek πρωτόπλαστος. This term appears in a
handful of the works of Bernard of Clairvaux, always in reference to Adam, and often with mention of Adam's sin and guilt.
See, e.g., *Letter VII to Adam the Monk*, Ep 7.3 (SBOp 7:33): "And
he said to the first man: Because you heeded the voice of your
wife rather than mine, the earth is cursed in your work" (*Et item
ad Protoplastum: Pro eo quod oboedisti voci uxoris tuae plus quam
meae, maledicta terra in opere tuo* [Gen 3:17]). See also SC 28.2:
"I recognize the form of denigrated nature, I perceive your
garments of skin, the condition of the transgressing first man"
(*Agnosco denigratae formam naturae; agnosco tunicas illas pelliceas,
protoplastorum peccantium habitum* [Gen 3:21]) (SBOp 1:193; CF
7:89).

[43] Ps-Bernard plays on two different meanings of the adjective
purus here when he uses *purus homo* ("mere human being") and

certain that he was deeply soiled with the contagion of sin. Neither God alone nor angel ought to have been sacrificed, because both, the former by nature and the latter by grace, show themselves to be impassible; the irrational creature was not sufficient for the magnitude of such a thing. Therefore it was necessary that someone both divine and human should be made the sacrifice: God, for the power of liberating, human, for the sufficiency of sacrificing; God, from mercy, human, from need. He was offered up, therefore, because *with him is propitiation, and with him is plentiful redemption.** *Ps 129:4, 7

He was offered up, because his inestimable love for humankind so decreed. *He was offered up because he so willed;** he was offered up to meet human need. *Isa 53:7

14. O human, *what do* you give back *to the Lord for all the things that he has* restored to you?[44]* He demands only love; only love suffices for him. Why do you not love the one who loves you? Let us love him, *because he has first loved us.** Do you want to hear the manner of his love, do you wish to learn its effect? *For God so loved the world that he gave his only begotten Son.*[45]* *God did not spare his own Son, but gave him up for us all.** Listen to this very Son. *Greater love has no man,* he says, *than this, that he lay down his life for his friends.**

*see Ps 115:12

*1 John 4:10

*John 3:16
*Rom 8:32

*John 15:13

---

puram hostiam ("pure sacrifice"). That *purus homo* should be translated "mere human being" is clear from rest of the sentence, since a "pure human being" would seem to denote one who is not "deeply soiled with the contagion of sin."

[44] Vulg: *Quid reddam Domino pro omnibus quae tribuit mihi.* Ps-Bernard has not only changed this verse from the first to the second person to fit the form of an address, but he has also changed both verbs (*reddam* and *tribuit*) into forms of the verb *retribuo,* which means "to give back, restore, or repay."

[45] See Bernard, Dil 1.1 (SBOp 3:119–21; CF 13:93). Bernard also quotes 1 John 3:16 and explains how when we think of God's love for us, we see that God is worthy of being loved in return, for his own sake. See also Aelred of Rievaulx, S 80 (CCCM 2B:319–28; CF 80), which appears to be the only homily in which he quotes 1 John 3:16. Aelred discusses the mode of God's love, which should inspire our reciprocal love for God.

Therefore O human, love your lover; love him not so much *in word or speech, but in deed and truth.** Love him with your whole heart, and with your whole soul, and with your whole strength, and with your whole mind.** Say, I will love you, Lord, my strength; Lord, my support and refuge, my deliverer.** O True Liberator, because you freed me, a poor man, from the mighty, and one powerless for whom there was no supporter,* and you freed my soul from destruction.** Behold the *best gift,*‡ mentioned before in the introduction of this chapter, about which Isaiah says, *A child is born to us, and a Son given to us,** and in another place, *How then also, with him, has God not given us all things?** If he gave to us him who *is all in all,*‡ then no doubt he gave all things to us with him. If therefore he is given to us, let us use this gift as our own,* *lest we give our honor to strangers and our years to the cruel.** For the present, let these things set down in the first part be useful.

*1 John 3:18

*Matt 22:37; Deut 6:5; 2 Kgs 23:25

*Ps 17:2-3

*Ps 71:12

*Sir 51:16
‡Jas 1:17

*Isa 9:6

*Rom 8:32
‡Col 3:11;
Eph 1:23

*Wis 2:6

*Prov 5:9

PART TWO:
That Jesus, the Son of God,
Gives Himself to Us in the Eucharist

Chapter Seven:
Concerning the Unspeakable and
Perpetual Clarity[46] of the Word Incarnate

15. The one who was first given to us as the price of redemption continues to give himself daily to us in

---

[46] The word here is *claritas*, which appears first in the Preface when Ps-Bernard states the question that the whole treatise is meant to address. How does Christ possess the splendor of clarity when he is hidden beneath the species of bread on the altar? In this chapter, Ps-Bernard turns his attention specifically to this question. According to the patristic and medieval theological tradition, clarity is the manifestation of divine glory. Here Ps-Bernard proceeds in an orderly way to show that

the Eucharist:[47] at first passible and exposed to sufferings, now impassible and *crowned with glory and honor;** then a man subject to death, now a man victorious over death; *then made a little lower than the angels,** now lifted up above all the angels. *As much as he has been made superior to the angels,* the apostle says, *he has inherited a name more excellent than theirs. For to which of the angels did the Father ever say, You are my Son, this day I have begotten you? And again, I will be a father to*

*Heb 2:7; Ps 8:6
*Heb 2:7; Ps 8:6

---

the clarity of the Eucharist is the radiance of the Godhead. God is clarity, and so the Word is clarity. The Word incarnate is also clarity; Christ's soul and glorified body possess clarity by union with the divine nature. Christ's body in the Eucharist, Ps-Bernard concludes, also possesses this clarity, the brilliance of God himself. This is the meaning of *claritas* in the patristic period; in medieval theology, *claritas* is also listed as one of the four gifts of a glorified body. It implies the other three, which are agility, subtlety, and impassibility. Clarity refers to the brilliancy of the glorified body (see Aquinas, ST III, qq. 54, 55).

[47] The word for Eucharist here is *viaticum,* whereas *Eucharistia* is used in the title of Part Two. The noun *viaticum* originally came from the Latin adjective equivalent to two Greek words: the first referred to a supper given to those setting out on a journey, and the second referred to the provision of all things necessary for a journey. In the Christian tradition, *viaticum* came to mean both the meal and provisions necessary for the journey of this life to the next. Originally, *viaticum* included such things as baptism, penance, confirmation, prayers, and good works. As early as the First Council of Orange in 441, *viaticum* referred more specifically to the Eucharist. By the time of the Council of Trent, that was its explicit usage. The Council explained the reason for the word's use for the Eucharist: "because it is the spiritual food by which we are supported in our mortal pilgrimage, as also because it prepares for us a passage to eternal glory and happiness" (Trent, Session 13, 11 Oct. 1551, in *Decretum de ss. Eucharistia,* chap. 3). In modern times, *viaticum* has acquired an even more exclusive usage: it primarily refers to the Eucharist given to those in danger of death as part of the Last Rites. For Ps-Bernard, its meaning would not yet have been so limited (see Augustin Joseph Schulte, "Viaticum," *The Catholic Encyclopedia* [New York: Robert Appleton Company, 1912]).

*Heb 1:4-6

him, and he shall be a son to me? And once more, when he brings the first-born into the world, he says, Let all the angels of God adore him.*

In this passage, dear priest of God, your desire seems to me chiefly to consist: you desire to be illuminated to some degree by that clarity that the Word incarnate possessed after the glorification of his assumed humanity, and *the willingness is within me, but*

*Rom 7:18
*Jas 1:5

I cannot find a way to do it of myself* unless he gives *who gives abundantly to all and does not reproach.** Whatever, then, he will deem worthy of giving, it will certainly be slothful for me not to write down, and it will be necessary for you.

16. First, observe what is written: *God dwells in light*

*1 Tim 6:16
‡Deut 4:24;
Heb 12:29

inaccessible,* and also, *Our God is a consuming fire.*‡ What each of these verses says refers to the divine essence, in which the Father is one with the Son and with the Holy Spirit, for in the Trinity there is no before or after, no greater or lesser; rather, all three persons are co-eternal and co-equal with each other.[48] For

*John 10:30

this reason, the Son says, *The Father and I are one.** If, then, they are one, they dwell in the same inaccessible light; they are the same consuming fire, and the same clarity, the same power, the same wisdom, the same majesty, the same eternity. And so the Son is from the Father, *God from God, Light from Light, True God from*

*Nicene Creed

True God.* Truly, he is the brilliance of Fatherly glory.[49]

---

[48] This Trinitarian formula originally comes from the sixth-century Athanasian Creed (Ps-Venantius Fortunatus, *Symbolum Athanasianum,* ed. B. Krusch, MGH auct. ant. 4, 2 [Berlin, 1885], 105–6).

[49] Bernard also uses this title for the Word in a discussion of equality within the Trinity (S In lab mess 3.4 [SBOp 5:224; CF 54:85]). The title comes from the opening line of a hymn attributed, with some confidence, to Ambrose of Milan (ca. 340–397): *Splendor paternae gloriae, / de luce lucem proferens, / lux lucis et fons luminis, / diem dies illuminans* ("Splendor of fatherly glory / bringing forth light from light / light of light and font of light

The apostle also speaks on this point: *who is the brilliance of his glory, the image of his substance.** There is certainly no doubt that this refers to the Father's glory and substance. Therefore the Son shines brightly in the same manner as the Father; better yet, the Son is the same brilliance that the Father is. Are these testimonies of the Son's clarity not sufficient for you? Or would you say, perhaps, that you prefer to delight in his clarity inasmuch as he is both God and man? If grace assist us, you will also not lack for testimonies about this aspect of Christ's clarity.

17. First, I want to warn you, lest you deem the Word's clarity to have been obscured by the human nature that God assumed. Listen to what is written: *God assumed a human nature; he did not abandon the divine nature: he assumed what he was not, remaining what he was.*[50] The angel said to Mary, *The Holy Spirit will come upon you, and the power of the Most High will overshadow you.** These words can be understood in this way: "The Holy Spirit will effect in you the incarnation of the Word, who is to become incarnate, by separating a little part of your flesh,[51] which will be animated and joined together[52] with the divine essence in the unity of this person."

*Heb 1:3

*Luke 1:35

/ day illuminating the day") (CPL 163, Hymn 2.1). Aelred of Rievaulx uses the first three verses of this hymn in a comparison between the glory of Moses' face after coming down from Mount Sinai and the glory that surrounded Mary when the Word Incarnate dwelt within her (see S 74.26, *On the Assumption of Holy Mary* [CCCM 2B:253; CF 80]).

[50] See Isidore of Seville, *De ecclesiasticis officiis* 1.26.18 (CCCM 113).

[51] See Bernard of Clairvaux, Miss 4.4 (SBOp 4:50–51; CF 18:49). Bernard also describes how God vivifies and appropriates a small portion of Mary's flesh in the incarnation.

[52] The Latin word *copulo*, which often means "join together in marriage."

But what is the reason for this overshadowing by the power of the Most High? Now this is truly extraordinary.[53] Unless the Virgin's flesh had been overshadowed by some hidden operation, it would never have been able to bear[54] the splendor of such majesty without being destroyed.[55] And so the Lord said to Moses, *No human being on earth will see me and live,** as if he were saying, "I am of such clarity in my divine nature that a human being made of mortal flesh will never be able to see me without being destroyed." And so it is that when Moses was beseeching the Lord with great perseverance, saying, *Lord, show yourself to me,* the Lord said, *Stand in the cleft of the rock, and when I have passed by, you will see my back, but you will not be able to see my face.** The Lord said this, designating his divinity by the face and his humanity by the back; Moses did not see the Lord's back with a corporeal vision, but he left the Lord's posterior for posterity to see.[56]

*Exod 33:20

*see Exod
33:18-23

The summit of this truth is when the glorious body of Christ, which is confected on the altar and distrib-

---

[53] The Latin word *praecipua,* which is the same word that Ps-Bernard uses in the title of his treatise to designate the mysteries of the Christian faith that he will discuss.

[54] The Latin word *ferre,* which means "to bear" both in the sense of "to suffer" or "endure," and "to carry." Both senses are intended here.

[55] See Bernard of Clairvaux, Miss 4.4 (SBOp 4:50–51; CF 18:49). Bernard also considers the meaning of the Angel's words, *"And the power of the Most High will overshadow you."* While Ps-Bernard's concern is to show that Mary needed to be overshadowed in order not to be overwhelmed by the clarity of the incarnation, Bernard underscores the hiddenness of the mystery that could be known only by Christ and Mary.

[56] I.e., Moses saw the incarnation with the eyes of his soul, but not with the eyes of his body. Ps-Bernard uses the limitation of Moses' vision to underscore that in the Eucharist, the Lord reveals the glory of his incarnation to bodily as well as spiritual eyes.

uted to the faithful in the Eucharist,* is made brilliant *viaticum
by the fire of divine ardor. For just as the most brilliant
purple stains the whitest wool, making the whole
color change into itself, so the soul animates, quickens,
and enlivens the whole body, and just as fire striking
iron ignites it, conveying its own radiance and heat,
causing the iron to glow, catch fire, and burn despite
its nature, so God deifies the one united to himself,
and after exalting him above all creatures, God glorifies this one with himself by the power of his purity
and the prerogative of his divinity.[57]

The Son gives the same testimony about himself,
saying, *I am the light that came into the world, yet the
people loved the darkness more than the light,** and again, *John 3:19
*I am the light of the world.** John says the same thing *John 8:12
explicitly: *He was the true light, which illuminates each
person coming into the world.** And as he was praying *John 1:9
before the passion, the Son spoke to the Father, saying,
*Glorify me, Father, with the clarity I had with you before
the world was made,** to which the Father replies, *And *John 17:5

[57] See Origen, *On First Principles* (Notre Dame: Ave Maria
Press, 2013), 2.6.6. Origen first employs the metaphor of iron
and fire for the union of Christ's human and divine natures
here, and it is taken up into the tradition of patristic and medieval theology. Origen also points out that the divine fire itself
essentially rests in the soul of the divine Word, and from him
warmth comes to all the other saints. Ps-Bernard develops this
aspect of the analogy further in terms of Christ's clarity, saying
that Christ is like the sun, and his clarity shines from his glorified humanity to all the saints in heaven. Note also that with
the two metaphors of color and fire, Ps-Bernard offers an account of the clarity of the Eucharist that parallels the nuanced
account Aquinas gives of the clarity of Christ's glorified body
(see Aquinas, ST III, q. 54, a. 2). Christ's soul possesses clarity
because of its union with the divine nature. After the resurrection, clarity flows from his soul into his body and also, as Ps-
Bernard develops here, to the Eucharist.

*John 12:28 *I have glorified, and I will glorify.** What is clearer?[58]
What is more manifest? What is more evident?
18. Draw clarity[59] from the Gospel, the clarity possessed by the God-man glorified according to his humanity, who, when the time approached to pass from this world to the Father, *took Peter, John, and James, and ascended to the summit of Mount Tabor, and was transfigured before them, and his face became bright as the sun, and his clothing as the snow, as no weaver on earth could make; Moses and Elijah also appeared, and when they looked upon the clarity of his countenance, they were unable to bear its brilliance, but fearing exceedingly and feeling terror in their*
*see Luke 9:28-36 *souls, they fell as if dead upon the ground.**

If so splendid an appearance, so radiant a brightness, deigned to appear to human eyes in such unbearable clarity, while still in a body exposed to corruption, with members not yet freed from mortality, we should believe that so great a clarity is in the Son of God in the form of man that he assumed, now glorified, now
*Ps 114:24 exalted above the *heaven of heavens,** now having *the name which is above every other name, so that at his name every knee shall bend in the heavens, on the earth, and under*
*Phil 2:9-10 *the earth,** now established *in the day of his strength, in the splendors of the saints,* when the Father says, as he fills his treasuries with delight and exultation, *Before*
*Ps 110:3 *the morning star I have begotten you.*[60]* There Christ

---

[58] Ps-Bernard employs word play with *claritas* and *clarius* that recalls his main intention in this chapter: to illuminate his audience by helping them to see Christ's own clarity. Ps-Bernard aims to mediate Christ's clarity to his audience with his words.

[59] Interestingly, Ps-Bernard extends the gift of clarity not only to Christ's glorified body in the Eucharist but also to Scripture.

[60] A disputed question in medieval exegesis of the transfiguration is whether Christ's body truly possesses clarity when he is transfigured, since it remains passible. A second question is whether the clarity possessed by Christ's glorified body after the resurrection is visible only to the eyes of the soul (see Aquinas, ST III, q. 45, a. 2). Ps-Bernard answers both questions here:

shines indeed, *in the day of his strength*, in the day of his eternity.

Absolutely no night breaks into this day, no darkness scatters it, no gloom dispels it in any way. There he is encircled by a sea of light, a boundless ocean of brilliance. There Christ himself shines like the sun into the golden vaults of heaven, and the mountains shine with his radiance. There the holy ones are filled with his light. And so the prophet says, *How wonderful was thy dawning over the everlasting hills!** And again, it is written, "In your orbit, O Lord, there is light that will never fail, there the souls of the saints rest in peace,"[61] and once more, "Holy and wonderful is the true light, providing light to those who have persevered in the battle's combat: they receive everlasting splendor from Christ, in whom the blessed perpetually rejoice."[62]

*Ps 76:5

19. See how true, how consonant are the testimonies about that blessed and unspeakable clarity in which Christ is or, rather, which Christ is: the clarity that cannot wane and cannot wax, because it is boundless,[63] it is eternal, it transcends all sense, it rises above all thought, and it exceeds all estimation. *Let the thoughts of man's heart be deep as they will, God will be exalted* in his incomprehensible clarity.* His clarity always re-

*Ps 64:7-8

Christ's body did possess clarity in the transfiguration, while remaining passible, and the clarity of Christ's glorified body, like the clarity of his transfigured body, is visible to both spiritual and bodily eyes.

[61] See Resp *In circuitu tuo* for Several Martyrs, in René-Jean Hesbert, ed., *Antiphonale Missarum sextuplex* (Brussels: Vromant, 1935), 3:3208 (hereafter Hesbert).

[62] Ant *Sanctum est verum lumen* for Several Martyrs (Hesbert 3:4768).

[63] In Part One, chap. 6, ¶7, Ps-Bernard uses the same word, *immensam*, to speak about the Word's boundlessness, which remains despite his wonderful abbreviation in the incarnation. Here, too, Ps-Bernard insists that the Word's boundless clarity does not lessen when he becomes abbreviated in the incarnation.

mains the same; it does not magnify with any drawing near, nor does it diminish with any moving away. His clarity has not lessened in his assumed humanity, nor in his glorified humanity has it surpassed what it is in God. This the prophet makes clear, saying, *But* *Ps 102:28 *you yourself are the same, and your years do not wane.** Habakkuk, also a prophet, says as he considers this light, *His splendor will be like the light; horns[64] are in his hands. There is his strength hidden, death will go before* *Hab 3:4-5 *his face,** openly indicating, moreover, that when his hands were fastened to the cross, although the sun

---

[64] After Tertullian's *Against the Jews* (CPL 33), the horizontal ends of Christ's cross were called his *cornua* or "horns" (10.41). *Cornua* also refer to the projections on an animal's head. Augustine brings the two meanings together in a sermon: "He's a bull: just look at the 'horns' of the cross" (S 19; CPL 284). The Venerable Bede takes up this double sense of the horns of the cross in his commentary on the book of Habbakuk: "But after he received the horns of the cross in his hands, there the power of his glory was confirmed, so that neither by terrors, nor by blows, nor by death itself was he able to be driven away from the heart of fidelity. . . . And the horns are in the hands of Christ, because he is the king of kings and the lord of lords" (CPL 1354). Here, therefore, Ps-Bernard draws upon an exegetical tradition that recognizes both senses of *cornua* in Habbakuk's verse, showing that when the horns of the cross were in Christ's hand, the strength of his clarity, though hidden, was not lessened. In addition, given the discussion that follows of the light of Christ's divinity shining forth from the cross, Ps-Bernard may also have in mind the horns of Moses, which were usually understood as "horns of light" streaming forth from his face after his descent from Mount Sinai. The medieval understanding of Moses as horned is based on Jerome's translation of the Hebrew word *qeren* as *cornuta*, in Exod 34:29. Jerome's translation is not a mistranslation, for *qeren* can refer to either "horns" or "rays of light." It seems clear that Jerome used the term metaphorically, and most medieval commentators understood Moses to have "horns of light" rather than "horns of bone": see Ruth Mellinkoff, *The Horned Moses in Medieval Art and Thought* (Berkeley, CA: University of California Press, 1970), 1–9, 76–93.

itself darkened[65] its rays lest it see Christ dying on the cross, the light of the divinity in Christ did not wane. And so it was spoken beforehand, *His splendor will be like the light.**   *Hab 3:4
You, O Jew, scoffing, said, *We saw him having no beauty or comeliness.** You saw with a bleary eye,[66] nay,   *Isa 53:2
with an eye completely blind, because at that time blindness fell upon Israel.[67]* Habbakuk, however, had   *see Rom 11:25
clear eyes: *and a people* of the Gentiles *wandering in darkness has seen a great light; in the region of death's shadow, a light for them has arisen.*[68]*   *Isa 9:2

20. The testimony from Habakkuk, therefore, agrees that the suffering of Christ's humanity did not diminish the light of his divinity; on the contrary, the conqueror of death by dying himself triumphed over death, and his death trampled your own death. *There*

---

[65] The Latin word, *obumbrasset,* is the same word used in Luke's account of the annunciation, to which Ps-Bernard draws attention in Part One, chap. 7, ¶17. Thus Ps-Bernard suggests that the sun "overshadowed" its rays not only because of the horror of Christ's death, but also because of his overwhelming clarity even on the cross.

[66] The language of bleary eyes first apears in Scripture in the Genesis description of Leah and Rachel: *But Leah was bleary eyed; Rachel was beautiful and well-favored* (Gen 29:17).

[67] Ps-Bernard adds a *tunc* and omits *in parte,* so altering Paul's statement. In the Letter to the Romans, Paul says that since the incarnation, blindness has fallen "in part" upon Israel until the fullness of the Gentiles comes into the church. Then, however, the natural branches (Israel) will be grafted back onto their own olive tree. Because blindness has only fallen in part, sight can be restored. Paul's main theme in this chapter is that Christians should not boast against the branches that have been broken off (the Jews), for God is able to graft them into the tree again; thus *in parte* is significant.

[68] Ps-Bernard introduces the word *gentium* into the quotation from Isaiah. While Isaiah designates a single entity, *populus,* which has moved from blindness into light, Ps-Bernard employs the partitive genitive to designate a more specific people, which has moved from blindness into light, a part of the whole *gentium.*

*Hab 3:4

*Jer 11:19

*Wis 2:20

*Luke 24:21

*Hab 3:4

*see Matt 12:29;
Luke 11:21, 22

*Ps 23:8, 10
‡Hab 3:5
†Hos 13:14

his power was hidden. His pitiful body, lifeless, parched, and bloodless, hangs on the cross; with his neck bent downward, his head barely clings to his low-hanging neck, with a bruised face, eyes mournful in death and half-closed, hands stretched out and fastened to the wood by nails. *There his power was hidden*, hidden from the Jews, hidden from his disciples. It was hidden from the Jews, who said, "*Let us wipe him out from the land of the living,* let us condemn Him to a shameful death.*" It was hidden from the disciples, who said, "*but we were hoping that he was the one who would redeem Israel.*" His splendor will be like the light, and he will have horns in his hands.* He withers on the cross, he shines forth in the air, he hangs on the gibbet, he gleams in the highest heaven.[69]

O holy Habukkuk, how well the splendor of his light shone, who shone previously to you so many ages ago! The *horns* of the cross are *in his hands*; but also his *hands* are on the *horns* of the cross. *There his strength is hidden*, but not in the presence of the dead.[70] There he crushed the iron bars, there he shattered the copper gates, there he manifests his strength, there that stronger man binds the strong man and snatches away the vessels[71] of the one who guarded *his own hall in peace.* There it is proclaimed, "*Who is the king of glory?*" There it is heard, "*The Lord, strong and mighty, the Lord, mighty in battle, the Lord of strength himself is the king of glory.* Death will go before his face.‡ O Death, I will be your death; Hell, I will be your bite.† Where is your*

---

[69] There is a certain word play here with *aret* (withers) / *aere* (air) and *claret* (shines forth) / *pendet* (hangs) / *splendet* (gleams).

[70] This is perhaps a reference to Christ's descent to hell prior to his resurrection. The Apostles' Creed refers to it, and it is alluded to in 1 Pet 3:19-20; 4:6.

[71] Ps-Bernard addresses his reader as *vas electionis* in the *Proemium*. The image is meant to suggest that of Christ overpowering the devil and snatching away the souls of the elect—the vessels—from hell.

victory, O Death? Where is your sting? Death has been
consumed in victory."*   *1 Cor 15:54, 55
The victor returns from the depths with a celebrated,
solemn procession. "*The devil goes*," he says, "*before his
feet.*"* *Now is the judgment of the world; now will the*   *Hab 3:5
prince of this world be cast out.* *His splendor will be like*   *John 12:31
the light*—*to illuminate those who sit in darkness and the*   *Hab 3:4
shadow of death.* The clarity of the Word incarnate,   *Luke 1:79
therefore, remains in his glorified humanity; it persists
in him who has been established at the right hand of
the Father. It will neither wane nor diminish with time,
it is darkened by nothing. It shines as much when it
is on the altar as in the height of heaven; nor does it
radiate less when it is in the hands of priests than
when it is in the bosom of the Father.

Chapter Eight:
Concerning the Dignity of the Priest

21. Therefore, always *boast, but in the Lord,** priest   *see 1 Cor 1:31;
of the most high God; consider your dignity, observe   2 Cor 10:17
your excellence with the eyes of the mind, ponder
your privilege, see your lot. Without doubt, *the lines
fell to you in magnificent things,* if you do not neglect
your *magnificent inheritance.** Heed how greatly your   *Ps 15:6
God has exalted you, how greatly before all creatures
he has elevated you. Let your prayer be pure, because
a place is given to your voice in heaven when you
stand with due observance at the sacred altar, when
you reach out to celebrate the most holy mystery of
the heavenly sacrifice. At the sound of your voice, at
your vivifying word, at your saving request, the highest Father, by whose command[72] all things subsist,
whom the angels praise incessantly,* to whom the   *see Rev 4:8
morning stars raise *shouts of joy,** whom the *Dominations*   *see Job 38:7

---

[72] Lit. "by whose nod."

*Eph 1:21;
Col 1:16
‡Ps 103:32
◊Ps 135:4

‡see Dan 3:40;
Mic 6:7
*Gen 4:2-4

*Gen 22:1-18
*Gen 14:18-20;
Ps 110:4;
Heb 5:5-10

*Ps 39:7-8

*Heb 9:12

*Exod 12
*John 1:29

*John 8:29

*John 1:33

adore, at whom the *Powers** tremble, *who looks upon the earth and makes it tremble,‡ who alone did great wonders,◊* the very same Father, I say, so immeasurable, entrusts his most sweet Son and places him in your hands; the Father hands over the Son from the highest heights and puts him in your fingers.[73] There, your holocaust is made fat, more than thousands of fat lambs and rams.‡

22. For Abel's gift was readily accepted,* but not in the same way; the sacrifice of the patriarch Abraham was especially pleasing,* but not to the same degree; the offering of Melchizedek was greatly approved,* but much less than this one. In short, what does the prophet say? *Sacrifice and offering you did not desire, holocaust and offering for sin you did not demand; then I said, "Behold, I come."** He said, *Not through the blood of goats or bulls, but through his own blood he entered once into the Sanctuary, acquiring eternal redemption.** All things in former times happened in figure. Here truth, there the figure; there shadow, here light; there clouds, here clarity; there the lamb of the law,* here the innocent lamb *who takes away the sins of the world.** For it is the true Son of God whom you, priest, sacrifice, whom you take in your hands, whom you consume with your mouth, whom you send into your body.

But it is not only his majesty that comes to you. The Son comes to you, but not without the Father. *The one who sent me*, he says, *is with me, and he has not left me alone.** The Son comes to you, but not without the Holy Spirit. For what does John say? *"He upon whom you will see the Spirit descending and remaining* is himself the Christ."* Upon others the Holy Spirit descends but does not remain always. Upon Christ the Spirit descends and assuredly will remain always. No less, the whole host of heavenly citizens is present. *Thousands of thousands*, it says, *ministered to him, and ten*

---

[73] There is a certain wordplay here: *deponit* (entrusts) / *imponit* (places) and *transmittit* (hands over) / *immittit* (puts).

thousand times a hundred thousand stood before him.* For although the angels are ministers of the Spirit, *having been sent to minister to those who receive the inheritance of salvation,** they nonetheless *see the face of the Father,*[74]‡ always standing before the face of his majesty, *upon which they desire to gaze.** The ones who thirst to enjoy him more delight and do not shrink from him.[75]

Do you believe, holy priest, that you are surrounded with such a light and are in the presence of such majesty? That you are in such a solemn arrival and assembly of the Trinity, and of the whole heavenly host? Do you judge that such clarity is present and belongs to the whole heavenly court? Doubtless you would not be able to bear[76] so great a thing unless *the power of the Most High overshadowed* your weakness in order that you might bear it.*

Chapter Nine:
That the Priestly Power is Greater than the Angelic Dignity

23. Take heed, therefore, as I said before, and always hold in mind and remember with perpetual recollection the grace that was uniquely conferred upon you by God, which was neither granted to angels nor conceded to

Margin references: *Dan 7:10 · *Heb 1:14 · ‡Matt 18:10 · *1 Pet 1:12 · *Luke 1:35

[74] This reference is also found in Bernard of Clairvaux: see Csi 5.4.8 (SBOp 3:472; CF 37:147), and "Sermons on Psalm 90 . . . Sermon Eleven, on Verse Eleven," in *Angelic Spirituality: Medieval Perspectives on the Ways of Angels,* ed. Steven Chase (Mahwah, NJ: Paulist Press, 2002), 110.

[75] See Adam of St. Victor's sequence for the Feast of All Saints, *Supernae matris gaudia.* The text given by Ps-Bernard reads, *fruuntur, nec fastidiunt, qui eo magis frui sitiunt,* while the sequence reads, *Fruuntur, nec fastidiunt / Quo frui magis sitiunt*: see Richard Chenevix Trench, ed., *Sacred Latin Poetry,* 3rd ed. (London: MacMillan, 1874), 325.

[76] See Part Two, chap. 7, ¶17. Once again, the Latin word *ferre* may intend both senses of *to bear* ("to endure" and "to carry"), given that the priest holds the Host in his hands.

other men. For the bread in your hands is transubstantiated[77] into the Body of the only-begotten Son of God; the wine is converted into the most holy Blood of our Lord Jesus Christ by your blessing.[78] The *seraphim*, greatly united in rank and charity of spirit, burn for the holy Trinity above all the other ranks. And so the *seraphim* are understood as burning, or enflamed.[79] For each order is determined by the name of its character, which it receives quite fully in its office.[80] Nevertheless, they do not outshine this privilege, so that they

---

[77] The Latin word is *transubstantiatur*, but its use here need not imply the precise doctrinal formulation that developed after Lateran IV, particularly as the word was in use well before the council, at least from the mid-twelfth century. See Hans Jorissen, *Die Entfaltung der Transsubstantiationslehre bis zum Beginn der Hochscholastik* (Münster, Westfalen: Aschendorffsche Verlagsbuchhandlung, 1965), 7–8, 11–44.

[78] The following discussion of the nine choirs of angels may help to explain in part the attribution of this work to Bernard of Clairvaux, whose writings contain frequent reference to the angels. Ps-Bernard's treatment of the nine angelic choirs shares several features with Bernard's. See Bernard, SC 19.2–6 (SBOp 1:109–11; CF 4:141–44); and Csi 5.4.7–10 (SBOp 3:471–75; CF 37:146–52). Like Bernard, Ps-Bernard closely follows Saint Gregory the Great's description of the choirs: see Gregory the Great, Homily 34 (CCSL 141:299–319); Hurst, trans., *Homilies*, 286–89. This homily in particular describes the roles of the nine angelic choirs; significant portions of this homily were used in the office of readings for the feast of Saint Michael. See, e.g., Lucca, Biblioteca Arcivescovile, MS 5. It seems unlikely that Ps-Dionysius is a major source for Ps-Bernard, as the ordering of the two hierarchies differs. Also missing is Ps-Dionysius's emphasis on the mediatory role of the higher orders in relation to the lower orders. See Ps-Dionysius, *The Mystical Theology and the Celestial Hierarchies* (Godalming, Surrey, UK: Shrine of Wisdom, 1949), 45–59.

[79] The association of the seraphim with fire is found in Isa 6:2-6 and also informs both Gregory's and Bernard's descriptions.

[80] The Latin word is *munere*, which could also be translated as "gift," or "offering." The word refers to the angels' offering to God, which each choir makes according to its specified office. See Bernard of Clairvaux, SC 19.5 (SBOp 1:111; CF 4:143).

should consecrate the Body and Blood of our Redeemer in a subordinate, created thing.

The *cherubim*,* to whom the fullness of knowledge belongs, also bear witness to this with their name, because they are intimately acquainted with everything concerning the heavenly mysteries; they are amazed that *wonderful knowledge was bestowed*[81] and that priestly power is outside of them, and that they are not able to do what the priest can do. The *thrones*,* who are of such dignity that God sits on them and through them decrees his judgments, do not have superior power in that in which priests are remarkable. The *dominations*,‡ although they have received lordship over the rest from the Lord;[82] the *principalities*,* even though they rule over the other subjects for themselves;[83] the *powers*,† who excel with loftiness of power; the *virtues** of the heavens, who restrain the *airy powers** with their virtue, lest they exercise all their wickedness on the human race; the archangels, though it belongs to them to announce the highest mysteries of the divine will to the lower spirits and by authority to send the same lower spirits to humans; the angels, although they *always* see *the face of the Father who is in the heavens:** these, I say, all the holy orders of the blessed spirits, although they fully enjoy beatitude, so that they lack nothing of the highest felicity, nevertheless revere the glory of the priest, admire his dignity, yield to his privilege, honor his power.

24. O ecclesiastical race, *royal priesthood, holy nation, people of possession, proclaim the virtues of the One who has called you out of darkness into his marvelous light** and his ineffable mystery. *You are the light of the world, you are the salt of the earth.** It is said to the Levites, *Be clean,*

Margin references: *Ezek 10; *Col 1:16; ‡Eph 1:2; Col 1:16; *Eph 1:21; Col 1:16; †Eph 1:21; Col 1:16; *Eph 1:21; *Eph 2:2; *Matt 18:10; *see 1 Pet 2:9; *Matt 5:13, 14

[81] From the Introit *Resurrexi* for Easter: see Hesbert, 80.

[82] The alliteration in *Dominationes* (Dominations), *dominium* (lordship), and *a Domino* (from the Lord) is, alas, diminished here.

[83] The connection between *principatus* (principalities) and *principentur* (rule over) is lost in the translation.

*Isa 52:11
*you who carry the vessels of the Lord.** It must be said to you, *"Be clean, you who* are *the vessels of the Lord."* [84]

*1 Cor 6:20
*Glorify and carry God in your body.** God *has chosen* you

*Ps 32:12
*as his own inheritance.** In you is buried that glorious and glorified body, which some time ago died in Jerusalem and was buried, lifeless. Certainly, that holy man Joseph was only willing to bury that body in a new tomb, a tomb in which no one had yet been laid;

*Matt 27:59, 60;
John 19:41
he took pains to *wrap the body in clean linen.**

Woe to you if you have not also laid that body in a new tomb, or at least one that has been made like new, that is, in a body inwardly clean from sin, or, if you have sinned, in a body made clean through penance and reparation! Woe to you, if you have not laid that body in clean linen, that is, in a conscience inwardly purified[85] and absolved from all uncleanness! Do not let *a pact between Christ and Belial*, an *agreement between God and idols*, a fellowship between light and darkness,

*2 Cor 6:15, 16
‡Rom 6:12
be in your body;* *let not sin reign in your mortal body,*‡ and thus you will consecrate a venerable tomb for Christ, a temple for the Holy Spirit. *"The temple which*

*1 Cor 3:17
you are," says the apostle, *"is holy to the Lord,"** and again, *"Or do you not know that our bodies are temples of*

*1 Cor 6:19
*the Lord, and that the Holy Spirit dwells in us?"** If this is said truly about anyone who has charity, a great deal more should be said about the priest, who is pleasing to God.

25. Consider and also take heed, faithful priest, with what diligence, with what vigilance the holy angels guarded the place of the tomb, when the Lord's body was already raised, renewed, and glorified; in what clarity, in what beauty of face and raiment they ap-

---

[84] See Acts 9:15. Ps-Bernard first addresses his reader as a *vas electionis* in the *Prooemium*.

[85] The Latin word is *defaecata*, which in addition to "purified" can also mean "set at ease." Ps-Bernard may also intend this second meaning with respect to the conscience.

peared to the holy women who were visiting the tomb and seeking the body. Without a doubt, you ought to know that if you have worthily handled this same body of the Lord—a body already above, reigning in the heavens in a glorious manner, and honored at the right hand of the Father—you will have prepared a clean and new tomb out of your body.* Even this constant guard of the angels[86] will not be lacking to you; they will preserve your soul, govern your body, and defend you against all your vices. And they will say to you and your like, *You will be called holy of the Lord, servants of our God.** Watch, therefore, that you do not touch that sacrifice except with *innocent hands and a clean heart.** Otherwise, he himself will say to you, *Do not touch me,** because your touch is pollution.

*see Matt 23:26-
28; Matt 27:60

*Isa 61:6

*Ps 23:4
*John 20:17

Chapter Ten:
Concerning the Meditation of the Priest, or Concerning His Preparation to Celebrate So Great a Mystery Worthily

26. Meditate, beloved priest of God, and let the meditation of your heart always be this, that John the Baptist—the forerunner of the Lord, the friend of the Bridegroom, the groomsman of the Bride, *a prophet,*

---

[86] The idea of the *custodia angelorum* was especially influential in the angelology of the later Middle Ages. Although Bernard does not mention the topic, it is discussed by Albert the Great (Albertus Magnus) (*Commentarii in II Sententiarum* 2 d. 11, a. 2–6), Alexander of Hales (*Summa Fratris Alexandri* 2.1.2), Bonaventure (*Commentaria in Sententiarum* 2 d. 11), and Thomas Aquinas (ST I, q. 113). While the role of ministering angels goes back to the gospel, the particular concept of *custodia* seems to be traceable to an Exposition on the gospel of Mark attributed to Jerome. In his commentary, Ps-Jerome allegorically explains the parable of the vineyard (Mark 12:1-12), describing the hedge as the *custodia angelorum* (*sepis est custodia angelorum*): see CPL 632:12.52.2.

*Matt 11:9;
Luke 7:26

*see Matt 11:11;
Luke 7:28

*see Matt 3:14

*Matt 16:19
*John 21:15-17

*Luke 5:8

*John 19:26-27

*1 John 1:1

and more than a prophet, sanctified in the womb, justified in the wilderness—that so great a one as this, and of such particular merit, having been made singularly holy,* trembles all over and does not dare to touch the sacred head of God but cries out with trembling, "Sanctify me, Savior."*[87] Meditate on this, that Peter— designated by the Lord the keeper of the keys to the kingdom of heaven,* appointed Shepherd of the sheep by his threefold confession of love,* and prefigured as the chief of the apostles—when in danger of death and with shipwreck looming, when he was in the presence of the Lord, utterly feared to approach him and wished rather to withdraw himself out of fear, saying, *Depart from me, Lord, for I am a sinner.**

Meditate also on John, that chosen and beloved disciple, who reclined upon the breast of the Lord at supper, the virgin[88] to whom Christ on the cross entrusted his Virgin Mother,* to whom likewise were revealed the heavenly secrets while still in mortal flesh—the same one has gloried above measure in what was merely heard and seen externally, and touched of the body of the Lord, saying, *That which was from the beginning, which we have heard, which we have seen with our eyes, which we have looked upon, and which our hands have touched, concerning the Word of life.**

If therefore these glorious rulers of the earth, these distinguished princes of the heavenly court, so feared publicly to touch the body of the Lord while it was not yet taken in glory to heaven, with how much more reverence, with how much fear and trembling, with what great chastity of body and purity of soul—now that the Lord's body is glorified and lifted up on high above all things, in the brightness of the glory of the

[87] Here Ps-Bernard quotes an antiphon to the cross attributed to Gregory the Great (*Liber Responsalis*, PL 78:744).
[88] For patristic references to the virginity of John the disciple, see Augustine's *Tractates on John*, Trac 124.7, and Jerome's *Book I against Jovinian*, chap. 27.

Father—ought the priest to confect it, to touch it, to take it in hand, and to take it into his own body?[89]

27. Wherefore *if you* (whoever may be a priest) *are offering your gift at the altar*, if you intend to celebrate that venerable and ineffable mystery *and you remember that your brother has something against you**—that great Brother, who is the Son of God by nature and *who gave us the power to be the sons of God*,* and his brothers through grace, who deigned to call us his brothers, speaking through the prophet, *I will speak your name to my brothers*,* and again after the resurrection: *Go! Speak to my brothers!** etc.—if this Brother has something against you, if you have offended his majesty by thought, word, or deed, if you have darkened the brightness of your innocence by some stain, if you have either an exceedingly sickly conscience or one less healthy—leave your offering there, defer the mystery, and go first to be reconciled to your Brother, through devoted contrition of the heart, through the pure confession of the mouth, through the hard wasting away of the body in penitence, and through fitting satisfaction. *Wash your bed every night*;* from every single sin cleanse your conscience.[90]

Ascend the tribunal of your conscience that you may sit in the place of Judgment; condemn yourself, and establish your guilt. Let the memory of your sin approach you as an accuser, let your own action be a witness against you, let your consent and delight make heavier your sin or guilt. Let everything accuse you; let nothing excuse you. Allow fear to come as an

*Matt 5:23

*John 1:12

*Ps 21:23
*Matt 28:10

*Ps 6:7

---

[89] The concern for priestly purity similar to the one evident here is reflected also in canons 14–18 of the Fourth Lateran Council.

[90] See Bernard of Clairvaux: "Have mercy on your own soul if you want God to have mercy on you. Drench your bed in tears night after night, and remember to water your couch with weeping [Ps 6:7]" (*Bernard of Clairvaux: Selected Works*, trans. G. R. Evans [New York: Paulist Press, 1987], 88) (Csi 16.29; SBOp 4:104).

executioner, and let the torturer crucify your guilt. Let the blood of the heart—that is, your tears—flow, and thus through proper judgment you will escape the penalty of divine Judgment, in accord with that saying of the apostle: *Because if we were to judge ourselves, we* _{*1 Cor 11:3} *would assuredly not be judged by the Lord.** Then, when you come to the altar, you will offer your gift, and *it will be more pleasing to God than a young calf producing* _{*Ps 68:32} *horns and hoof.**

Chapter Eleven:
That the Rite of Purification in the Law
Teaches Zeal for Purity

28.[91] And from the rite of the priest under the Law who is about to enter the Holy of Holies: *Make for yourself a wash-basin from the mirrors of the women who kept* _{*Exod 38:8} *watch at the door of the tabernacle,** so that if you discover any stain on your body while you are washing, you may wash it off. Take the washbasin as the Sacred Scriptures themselves; understand the women keeping watch at the mouth of the tabernacle as the holy souls keeping watch at the entrance of the kingdom of heaven. The mirrors are the examples of the saints,

---

[91] The following paragraph draws on the material in Gregory the Great's homily on Luke 10:1-7 (Homily 17.10 [CCSL 141:124–25]; Hurst, trans., *Homilies* [Homily 19], 134–50, esp. 141–42). Hurst notes, "This notion of cleansing the mirror of our souls of the stains which are on it as a result of sin, so that we may recover the divine likeness to God in which we were originally created, was picked up by Saint Bernard in the early middle ages" (150 n. 6). In the same note Hurst lists three additional sources for this topic: Cuthbert Butler, *Western Mysticism* (London: Constable & Co., 1922), 95–101, 142–45; Étienne Gilson, *The Mystical Theology of Saint Bernard* (New York: Sheed & Ward, 1940), 19, 45–59, 70–74, 92–99; and G. B. Ladner, *The Idea of Reform* (Cambridge, MA: Harvard University Press, 1959), 4, 74–107.

or the testimonies of Scripture; in these the souls of the just examine themselves as if in a mirror, and they correct whatever deformities they find in themselves. Spend your time, therefore, continually in holy meditations on these divine letters, delight yourself in them as if you were being illuminated by divine light, and examine yourself completely there, as if in a mirror. If you find something in you that is evil, correct it; something upright, maintain it so; something deformed, reform it; something beautiful, cultivate it; something healthy, preserve it; something weak, strengthen it. Read the precepts of the Lord without tiring, love them insatiably, fulfill them effectively, and through these, once you are sufficiently instructed, discern what it is you must guard against and what it is you must pursue.

29. Behold, you know now the first steps to avoiding evil and doing good; if you follow them, *the Lawgiver will bless you*, and with him as your guide *you will advance from strength to strength,** and *God himself will be your protector and a place of refuge so that you might be saved,** and he will say to you, *Behold, I am with you all the days of your life, until the end of the age.** Truly he will be with you, because he will give himself in the Eucharist* so that you may not fail on the journey, until he should fully refashion you in your homeland. Therefore examine yourself in the manner above, and accordingly eat of this bread of the holy Eucharist and drink from the chalice.

*Ps 83:8

*Ps 30:3
*Matt 28:20

*viaticum

Chapter Twelve:
Concerning the Three Ways of Receiving the Body and Blood of the Lord

30. Concerning this most sacred bread and the venerable chalice—that is, the life-giving Body and Blood of the Lord—a discerning priest ought not to

be ignorant that there are three ways of receiving.[92] One is both a sacramental and spiritual receiving, and this is real, holy, and sanctifying, blessed and beatifying, living and life-giving. The second is only spiritual, and this nonetheless confers grace, increases virtues, and accumulates merit. The third is only sacramental, and this is damnable and condemning, hateful to God, both separating us from him and by no means beatifying us. Any religious priest who has been properly

*see Matt 22:11 adorned with his *wedding garment**—that is, charity— and who is guilty of no mortal sin, who approaches the altar of God and solemnly celebrates the sacred mysteries, receives the holy Eucharist spiritually and sacramentally. In the same manner, and by the same merit, each of the faithful who from the hand of the priest partakes of the Eucharist itself receives the sacrament.

However, the priest is himself distinguished in comparison with others by the singular prerogative that he has the power to confect the Eucharist and receive it daily—so long as no fault or weakness impedes him—while, for others, it is permitted to communicate only at certain times from the hand of the priest.[93] All the faithful receive spiritually only inasmuch as they

---

[92] Several authors contemporary with Ps-Bernard also refer to the *triplici sumptione* (the three ways of partaking) of the Eucharist. See, for example, Hugh of St. Victor, *Summa Sententiarum Septum Tractatibus Distincta*, Tr 6.3, 7 (PL 176:140A–40D and 143B–44C). Peter Lombard writes of "two ways of eating" in *Sentences* 4 d.9.1 (55). See also Hugh of St. Victor, *De Sacramentis* 2.8.7.

[93] Before the fourth century, Christians tended to receive Communion at every celebration of the Eucharist, and certainly at least every Sunday. Very soon after Constantine, however, the frequency of Communion began to diminish, so that already in 506 the Synod of Agde required the faithful to receive Communion a minimum of three times a year (implying that people were receiving it less often than that). The Fourth Lateran Council in 1215 set a new minimum of once a year, at Easter.

are members of the church and persevere in charity, for though they do not touch the sacrament with their mouth, they nevertheless obtain for themselves the power of the sacrament—that is, the remission of sins, the infusion of spiritual grace—through faith and through union with the church. One who while abiding in mortal sin presumes to communicate receives only sacramentally, but such a one is a fellow of the betrayer, Judas, and *it would be better if that person had not been born,** unless he or she repents and makes satisfaction in a way worthy of God. *Mark 14:21

31. About the first way of receiving, which is sacramental and spiritual, the Lord says: *He who eats my flesh and drinks my blood remains in me and I in him,** *John 6:57 and again, *He who eats me shall live by me.** About the *John 6:58 second, which is solely spiritual, once more the same Lord says, *The flesh profits nothing, it is the spirit that gives life,** as if he had said, "If you perceive only the *John 6:64 carnal reception apart from grace, it profits nothing; on the contrary, it does harm, but the spiritual apart from the carnal gives life to you." About the third, which is solely sacramental, the apostle says, *He who eats and drinks unworthily, eats and drinks judgment unto himself, not discerning*[94] *the body of the Lord,** which is to *1 Cor 11:29 say, "not distinguishing the body of the Lord from other foods." This distinction of the Lord's body from other foods is beneficial, because when we receive other foods, we incorporate them into our body, but when we receive the body of the Lord in food, if we do this worthily, we are incorporated into the Lord;[95]

---

[94] The Vulgate's *dijudicans*, translated here as "discerning," also carries with it a sense of "judging," as in "judging by discernment," and therefore resonates with the notion of *judicium*, translated "judgment," in the preceding clause.

[95] This idea is first found in Augustine, S 227: *Si bene accepistis, vos estis quod accepistis* ("If you receive well, you are what you receive").

*1 Cor 6:17

*viaticum

*Matt 28:20

*Deut 30:14
*John 1:1
*see Rom 10:8

indeed, we pass over altogether into God, because *he who cleaves to God is one spirit* with him.* Happy is the wayfarer who is restored by such a provision for the journey,* which securely leads him back on the way and transports him into his homeland.

32. Therefore, the first way of receiving corresponds to the priests themselves, who honor their ministry by a worthy execution of their office; through them alone the dispensation of reception belongs to the other faithful. For they have the keys of this sacrament[96] who are the true mediators between God and humankind, the voice and organ of the holy church, who offer to God the prayers of the people and carry back mercies. O how faithful a Promiser![97] How true a Fulfiller of Promises! How bountiful a Giver! You have said, "Lord Jesus, *Behold I am with you always, until the end of the age."** Truly you have said these words. *"The word is near,* says Scripture, *in your mouth, and in your heart."** The word that was in the beginning with God* vouchsafes to be with humankind until the end of the age: *It is in your mouth, it is in your heart.**

[96] See Matt 16:19. In the context of the Eucharist specifically, see Canon 1 of the Fourth Lateran Council (1215): *Et hoc utique sacramentum nemo potest conficere, nisi sacerdos, qui fuerit rite ordinatus secundum claves ecclesiae, quas ipse concessit apostolis et eorum successoribus Iesus Christus* ("And no one can confect this sacrament, except a priest who has been rightly ordained according to the keys of the Church, which Jesus Christ himself gave to the apostles and to their successors"). The issue of the keys and the sacraments was a live one in the 12th century; see Paul Anciaux's *La théologie du Sacrement du Pénitence au XIIᵉ siècle* (Louvain: E. Nauwelaerts, 1949).

[97] Augustine seems to be the earliest to use the phrase *fidelis promissor*. See his *Confessions* 9.3.5 (*Sancti Augustini Confessionum libri XIII*, ed. Lucas Verheijen, CCSL 27 [Turnhout: Brepols, 1990], 135) and his (dubiously attributed) *Sermones* 178. Berndt Hamm discusses Augustine's theology of *promissio* and Bernard's appropriation of Augustine on this topic in *Promissio, Pactum, Ordinatio: Freiheit und Selbstbindung Gottes in der scholastischen Gnadenlehre* (Tübingen: Mohr Siebeck, 1977), 8–22.

What could be nearer? What could be more inward? It is in your mouth: Therefore *may his praise be always in your mouth.** It is in your heart: Therefore *confess him with uprightness of heart** and *do not forget his benefits.* What are his benefits? *He atones for all of your iniquities, heals all of your infirmities, redeems your life from destruction, crowns you with mercy and compassion, satisfies with good things your desire,* giving his very self to you in the Eucharist.* *Your youth shall be renewed like the eagle‡* in the resurrection of the just, when he will give himself anew as a reward. In the final part, we will continue with the duty of writing concerning this reward, which he himself will deign to give.

*Ps 33:2

*Ps 118:7

*viaticum
‡Ps 102:2-5

PART THREE:
That Christ Gives Himself to Us
as a Reward in Heaven

Chapter Thirteen

33. This is Aristotelian: "Everything sensible that is posited outside of the senses is unknown."[98] This is divine: *What eye has not seen, nor ear heard, nor has it arisen in the heart of man, these are the things which God has prepared for those who love Him,** and that saying, *Eye has not seen, O God, apart from you, what things you have prepared for those who love you.** And John says, *No*

*1 Cor 2:9

*Isa 64:4

---

[98] Aristotle, *Topica* 5.3, 131b20. It is not clear whether Ps-Bernard means to contrast the Aristotelian teaching with that expressed in Isaiah and the First Letter to the Corinthians about the things God has prepared for those who love him. He could be arguing for a consistency between the two, since the quotation from Aristotle points out that things that are in themselves able to be sensed but have not actually been sensed are unknown. The things that God has prepared for those who love him are just such things, but with the help of Scripture—as the author points out at the end of the paragraph—the faithful Christian really can understand something about God through the mediation of created things.

*John 1:18;
1 John 4:12

*1 John 1:5

*2 Cor 5:7

*Rom 1:20

*Wis 3:1

*Symb Athan

*one has ever seen God.** What then? If things invisible to the eyes, inaudible to the ears, and inscrutable to the heart have been promised as the rewards of life, and if no one has ever seen God who is light* and the reward of the just, who then will dare to talk of the unheard and the utterly unknown? Who will presume to speak of the unspeakable? One thing I know: however great are those ineffable things, so much more are they desired, and everything that is desired is not able to be compared to them.

It is true according to the apostle that as yet *we walk by faith, and not by sight,** and that *the invisible things of God from the creation of the world are understood through the things which are made.** However much it is agreeable that we may feebly, from the similitude of things that belong to the senses, attempt to say something of the ineffable good promised to the faithful and blessed, we plainly presume nothing from our heart but draw what testimony we can from the Holy Scriptures.

34. It cannot reasonably be doubted by any wise person that after this life *the souls of the just are in the hand of God.** The souls of the reprobate, however, fall into suffering, according to which, *Whoever has done good works will enter into eternal life; but whoever has done what is evil will enter into the everlasting fire.** There is, therefore, a twofold motive of beatitude for the elect: one, the avoidance of punishment; another, the attainment of glory. Something must be mentioned briefly concerning the punishment of the wicked, in order that once we have considered this, the glory of the good may be judged greater, since the dignity of no thing is better declared than if the depravity of its contrary is not passed over in silence. *From the opposite vice a more charming power of beauty shines forth,* says Isidore.[99]

---

[99] Although the attribution to Isidore is now lost, the quotation is similar to a phrase preserved in the writings of Bernard of Clairvaux. In a letter concerning the duties of a bishop, Bernard writes, "It seems to me appropriate here to take a look at pride

O human being, consider all the punishments of the world and compare them to those of Gehenna. All of them together will be light. Furthermore, the cleansing fire, which is not that of Gehenna and which tortures according to measure, surpasses all worldly torments. Thus Augustine said concerning the Psalter, *Lord, do not accuse me in your fury, nor seize me in your wrath;** that is, let me not be among those to whom you will say in Judgment, *Go, cursed ones, into the everlasting fire.** Do not chastise me in your displeasure, that is, let me not have need of purifying fire, which is also called purgative, since it is more grievous than all that which a human being can suffer in this life. While many villainous people atone for their crimes through very diverse tortures, many people have also turned to the Lord through immense and excruciating torments.[100]

*Ps 37:2

*see Matt 25:41

Chapter Fourteen:
Concerning the Punishments of Hell

35. Hell, on the other hand (as can be shown from the proper authorities), has nine infamous punishments besides the innumerable other evils that it contains, whence this statement: "Hammer and stench, along with worms, fire, and cold, the vision of demons, darkness, shame, fiery chains."[101] There will be in that

---

as well, to see how the beauty of the virtue is brought out by the opposing vice" (*On Baptism and the Office of Bishops* [=Ep 42] 19, trans. Pauline Matarasso, CF 67 [Kalamazoo, MI: Cistercian Publications, 2004], 58; SBOp 7:114).

[100] This is a paraphrased reference to Augustine's interpretation. For the complete argument, see *Expositions of the Psalms 33–50*, trans. Maria Boulding, vol. III/16 (Hyde Park, NY: New City Press, 2000), 37.3.

[101] Within the context of Ps-Bernard's treatise this list of nine punishments meted out by the demons corresponds to the nine orders of angels (seraphim, cherubim, thrones, dominions, principalities, powers, virtues, archangels, angels) that he mentions

place inextinguishable fire, incomparable cold, immortal worms, intolerable stench, repeated striking of the hammer, dense and palpable darkness, where no order but rather eternal horror dwells, and where the transgressions of all to all are made known. There will be the faces of the demons, which seem to glow perpetually in the fire and compared to which nothing in this world is more horrifying or dreadful. There will be also fiery chains binding every limb. There, I say, is such a fire that every river collected into one could not extinguish it.

Thus we read in Matthew, *There will be there weeping and gnashing of teeth.** For smoke from the fire incites weeping of the eyes; the cold, gnashing of teeth. If a volcano were to be set there, it would turn to ice. The wretched rove about, having been condemned to these miseries; first from the flame into the cold, then from the cold into the flame, seeking a remedy for their contrary sufferings in contrary conditions, which no less torture them.[102] Thus blessed Job says, *They will pass from the cold of snow to heat beyond measure.**

36. In that place are immortal worms, snakes, and dragons, dreadful in appearance and hissing, which

*Matt 8:12

*Job 24:19

---

earlier in Part Two (chap. 9, ¶23). As each angel has its role in God's creation, so are the demons used correspondingly to chastise those in hell. The list of nine punishments is further attested by a number of 12th- and 13th-century authors, where it appears to have been an easily memorized list for use in preaching. Caesarius of Heisterbach for instance relates them in a helpful rhyming verse: *pix, nix, nox, vermis, flagra, vincula, pus, pudor, horror* (tar, snow, night, worm, whips, chains, gall, shame, dread) (*Dialogus Miraculorum—Dialog über die Wunder*, trans. Nikolaus Nösges and Horst Schneider, FC 86, vol. 5 [Turnhout: Brepols, 2009], 12.1).

[102] This is similar to the concept of *contrapasso* ("suffer the opposite"), well known in reference to the punishment of souls in Dante's *Inferno*. See for further detail the article "Contrapasso," in *The Dante Encyclopedia*, ed. Richard Lansing (New York: Garland Publishing, 2000).

live in the fire like fish in water. They punish the wretched and especially rove about and gnaw their members, against which they war specifically for their sins,* namely the genitals for carnal excesses, the palate, throat, and stomach for gluttonies, and likewise concerning every other member. Thus that saying of Wisdom: *By those things through which one sins, by these one is also tormented.** And thus Isaiah: *Their worm shall not die, and their fire shall not be quenched.** Moreover, a rank stench, which torments no less than the flame, streams forth from the fire. Thus likewise Isaiah, *Instead of a sweet smell, there will be a stench,** and the psalm: *Fire, brimstone, a wind of violent storms, will be the portion of their cup.** It calls the emission of smoke and stench *a wind of violent storms* because smoke and stench blow forth from the fire furiously after the fashion of a violent storm. The wretched are struck, so to speak, with scourges and hammers unceasingly by demons forcing them to confess their offenses, so that the demons, who were provokers of evils here, should also be torturers of the same evils there. Hence Solomon: *Torments are prepared for mockers.** Indeed the demons open their mouths over the wretched in derisive laughter saying, *Well done! Well done! Our eyes have seen it,** because they despised the fellowship of the nine orders of angels.[103]

*see Rom 7:23

*Wis 11:17
*Isa 66:24

*Isa 3:24

*Ps 10:7

*see Prov 19:29

*Ps 34:21

---

[103] Ps-Bernard's treatise ends here abruptly. While he had promised at the end of the second part to continue his exposition in regard to the reward of heaven, very little of the third part is devoted to that discussion. While it is always possible that the last section of the treatise has been lost, perhaps the author decided to take his own advice when he asked, "who then will dare to talk of the unheard and the utterly unknown?" (3.33).

Tractatus de statu virtutum humilitatis, obedientiae, timoris, et charitatis.
A Treatise on the State of the Virtues[1]

Preface

By the inspiring grace of him who blows where he wills and when he wills* and who makes eloquent the tongues of infants,* I desire, if I may, to bring together in a simple discourse certain things concerning the varying states of the virtues that are to be discovered through reading, and others that I heard from my teachers, adding still others if they perhaps come to mind that are not repugnant to faith and are strengthened by reason. Let the Paraclete, therefore, who preceded all things by breathing,* follow through all things, illumine the heart, uncover obscure things, and provide power. May he do this to his glory, to my advantage, and to the growth of novices, who from the mountain of pride have descended into the valley of weeping,* those who *meditate day and night upon the law of the Lord.** But since humility is the mother of the virtues, and the humility of human beings is not from human beings but is from above, let us begin with the humility of him who says, *Learn from me because I am meek and humble of heart.**

*see John 3:8
*see Ps 8:2; Matt 21:16
*see Gen 1:2
*see Ps 83:7
*Ps 1:2
*Matt 11:29

[1] Translated from PL 184:791–812.

79

PART ONE:
On Humility

1. Christ, *since he was in the form of God, did not consider it robbery to be equal to God, but emptied himself, taking the form of a servant.*[2]* He emptied himself, I say, so that he might become less than the Father, less than himself, *less than an angel,** so that he might be subject to human beings, indeed both to Joseph as the one who reared him and to holy Mary as his mother, according to that which is written: *And he was subject to them.** He emptied himself likewise so that he might become not only a man, but also a poor man. Indeed he hungered, he thirsted, he was tired—but because he willed to be.[3] Finally, he emptied himself to the point of derision, reproach, flogging; *like a sheep, he was led to the slaughter, and like a lamb before the shearer he did not open his mouth.** Behold the one *handsome in*

*Phil 2:6-7

*Ps 8:5; Heb 2:7

*Luke 2:51

*Isa 53:7;
see Acts 8:32;
Jer 11:19

---

[2] Saint Paul's description of Christ as "in the form of God" (*in forma Dei*) but also "taking the form of a servant" (*formam servi accipiens*) is understood by Ps-Bernard to refer to the incarnation of the second Person of the Trinity, the Word. Christ is *in forma Dei* insofar as he as the Word of God subsists in the divine nature from all eternity. On the other hand, Christ took on the "form of a servant" insofar as he as Word assumed a human nature in his person, thereby becoming a human being.

[3] In medieval Christology, these qualities were numbered among the things "coassumed" by the Word of God when he became incarnate. The word "coassumed" refers to those things not essential to human nature but assumed by the Word along with his human nature specifically for the sake of accomplishing salvation. Human beings were understood to be subject to hunger, thirst, fatigue, and, above all, death, only as a consequence of sin, and so these things were considered to fall outside of human nature. Given that Christ assumed a human nature uncorrupted by sin, the fact that he was subject to these defects was understood to be the result of an act of will on his part. See Thomas Aquinas, *Summa Theologiae, Latin Text and English Translation,* 61 vols. (1964; Cambridge, UK; New York: Cambridge University Press, 2006) (hereafter ST), III, qq. 7–15, esp. q. 14, a. 3.

form beyond the sons of men, *without beauty or comeliness!*[4]* *His face was as if it were hidden from [God] and despised, for which he was not respected by men,* but condemned with the unjust, *as if he were leprous, stricken, and humiliated by God. He was wounded because of our sins, bruised because of our iniquities; the chastisement of our peace was upon him, by whose bruises we have been healed.* *

O, the ineffable mercy of God, *who did not spare his own Son, but delivered him up for us all!* * He was born for us and dwelled in the world for us and died for us. He was poor and humble in conduct, poor and humble on the cross; he partook of our redemption, dispensing his own so generously that our way of living might be according to his life, and our redemption might be in his death.

2. Behold the incomparable humility of God! Incomparable, because it does not admit a worthy comparison; inestimable, because it is not able to be measured; ineffable, because it cannot be explained with words: that the God and Lord of all should become a man and the servant of all, that the invisible should be seen, that the Lord, *the bread of angels*[5] *

*Ps 44:3
*Isa 53:2

*Isa 53:3b, 4b-5

*Rom 8:32

*Ps 78:25

---

[4] See Augustine, *In Iohannis epistulam ad Parthos tractatus* IX.9 (PL 35:2052). Ps-Bernard follows Augustine in considering Ps 44:3 and the Servant Song of Isa 53 together, though with an interesting difference. In his homily Augustine focuses at length on the apparent contradiction between the psalm's description of Christ as "handsome in form beyond the sons of men" and the statement of Isa 53:2 that "we saw him, and he had neither beauty nor comeliness" (*vidimus eum, et non habebat speciem neque decorem*). In the end he resolves this tension by pointing to Phil 2:6-7: Christ was handsome because he was "in the form of God," but he emptied himself of this by "taking the form of a servant." Ps-Bernard elides these two verses into one sentence precisely in order to magnify the tension, in which is seen the extent to which Christ humbled himself.

[5] For the use of the phrase "bread of angels" (*panis angelorum*) in reference to Christ, see Augustine, *In Iohannis evangelium tractatus* 13.3.4 (PL 35:1494); S 196, 3.3 (PL 38:1020). Augustine

would be nourished, that the power of the heavens should be made weak, that life should die. The cause of this mystery is the justice and mercy of God. Surely pride had cast humanity down, and neither the human being who owed nor the angel who did not owe was able to satisfy God worthily—but no other creature was suitable for this task.[6] Therefore mercifully and justly God was made man: mercifully indeed with respect to God, who owed nothing to humanity except punishment, and justly concerning humanity, because human beings had sinned against God. [Thus God was made man] in order that his humility would humiliate the proud, and that his wisdom would illuminate the blind and rouse the indolent.[7]

---

frequently draws a parallel between the manna that came down from heaven to feed the Israelites during their wanderings in the wilderness and the incarnation of the Word described in the beginning of the gospel of John. See Bernard of Clairvaux, *De laude novae militiae ad milites templi liber* 6.12 (hereafter Tpl) (SBOp 3:224–25; CF 19:146–47); S *In nativitate domini* 2.4 (SBOp 4:254; CF 51:110). Also Aelred of Rievaulx, *De Jesu puero duodenni* 2.12 (CCCM 1:259; CF 2:16).

[6] On the debt owed by human beings due to sin and the satisfaction that could only be provided by the God-Man, see Anselm, *Cur Deus Homo* 1.5: *Quod redemptio hominis non potuit fieri per aliam quam per Dei personam* ["How the redemption of man could not be effected by any other than a divine person"]. See also *Cur Deus Homo* 2.6: *Quod satisfactionem per quam salvatur homo, non possit facere nisi deus-homo* ["How no being, except the God-man, can make the satisfaction by which man is saved"] (*Pourquoi Dieu s'est fait homme*, ed. and trans. René Roques, SCh 91 [Paris: Éditions du Cerf, 2005]).

[7] The phrase "rouse the indolent" is a translation of the Latin *frigidos igniret*, which could also be translated along the lines of "make red-hot the cold." In this case, it might be a reference to the warning in Rev 3:16 against being lukewarm. As translated here, this teaching seems to correspond to the multiple warnings against indolence or idleness in the Rule of Saint Benedict (hereafter RB), as well as the Rule's understanding of the power of Scripture to rouse the hearts of those who read it. For an instance of the latter, see RB Prol. 8-13, while for examples of the former, see RB 4.38; 18.24; and 48.1 (*RB 1980: The Rule of*

For he is *the way, the truth, and the life.** The way *John 14:6
especially of conversion, the truth of teaching, the life
of beatitude. He is the way without which we either
cannot move or move wrongly, the truth without
which we learn either nothing or only evil things, and
the life in which we live well and without which we
live entirely wickedly. For he is *the power of God, and
the wisdom of God,** and because he is the power of God, *1 Cor 1:24
he provides the power for his own passing through
any adversities, and because he is the wisdom of God,
he imparts understanding.

3. But behold, it comes to mind that the angel fell
through pride and did not descend from heaven. That
angel fell to his own ruin and the ruin of those who
belong to him; Christ descended to the exaltation of
his elect. Pride made the devil from the angel; the
humility of Christ made sons of God from the children
of the devil.* The proud devil fell from heaven into *see Gal 3:26;
hell with his own; humble Christ, having returned 1 John 3:2;
from the dead, ascended into heaven with his own. Ps 81:6
You see, therefore, how great is the elevation of humanity without the merit of humanity in the one person of Christ, and the humility of God without the
debt of God. Charity without limit! Example without
parallel! If, therefore, God is humbled on earth, why
thus far is man proud, who is *dust and ashes,** *maggot* *Sir 10:9
*and rottenness,** extolled today and not found tomor- *Job 25:6
row? He moreover who is proud on this earth, where
Christ was found humble, puts himself before Christ.[8]
But even so, *if he should ascend all the way to heaven by*

Saint Benedict in Latin and English with Notes, ed. Timothy Fry
[Collegeville, MN: Liturgical Press, 1981] [hereafter Fry]).

[8] See Ps-Bernard, *Instructio sacerdotis seu tractatus de praecipuis
mysteriis notrae religionis* (*Instruction for a Priest: A Treatise on the
Principal Mysteries of Our Religion* 1.6.9 [PL 184:778B; above,
p. 43]). There the author (who may not be the same as the author
of this treatise) cites the same passages from Sirach and Job to
the same effect, and also argues in a similar way that those who
are proud seek to exalt themselves above Christ.

pride, and his head should touch the clouds, he will be lost

Job 20:6-7 in the end to a dung heap. And where he climbs more
highly before humankind, he falls lower into ruin
before God. But where true humility descends more
humbly before humankind, it ascends more highly
see Luke 16:15 before God. Lowly humility is the friend of God, and
every true friend of God ascends, according to that
*Luke 14:10 which is written: *Friend, move up higher*—whence,
indeed, every humble person without doubt ascends,
since true humility does not in any way know a fall.
On the contrary, humility is always in the lowest
depths and hates its own excellence. For if humility
and pride are opposites, then while pride is love of
one's own excellence, humility is rightly contempt of
one's own excellence.[9] Just as pride is a vice by which
humans having been blinded to themselves take pleasure in themselves (though even in this they displease
God and humankind), so humility is a virtue by which
humans having been revealed to themselves displease
themselves, in which they truly please both God and
human beings.

4. However, there is a humility for beginning, another
for progressing, and another for perfection—a beginning in novices, a progressing in those who are fighting well, and a perfection in those who are meriting.
There is a humility that is sufficient, another that is
abundant, and another that is superabundant. Sufficient humility is that by which one subjects oneself to
a greater person and does not give preference to oneself over one's equal. Abundant humility is that by

---

[9] The definition of pride as "love of one's own excellence"
(*amor excellentiae propriae*) is the same given in Augustine, *De
Genesi ad litteram* 11.14.18 (*De Genesi ad litteram libri duodecim*,
ed. Joseph Zycha, CSEL 28/1 [Vienna: Austrian Academy of
Sciences, 1894], hereafter Gen ad litt). It is also cited, alongside
this same definition of humility, in Bernard of Clairvaux, *De
moribus et officio episcoporum* 5.19 (Mor [=Ep 42]) (SBOp 7:114–15;
CF 67:58). See also Bernard of Clairvaux, *Liber de gradibus humilitatis et superbiæ* 4.14 (hereafter Hum) (SBOp 3:27; CF 13:42).

which one subjects oneself to one's equal and does not give preference to oneself even over a lesser person. <Superabundant [humility], however, is that by which one subjects oneself even to a lesser person.>[10] But that humility that is sufficient, by which one begins to confess one's sins by repenting and to subject oneself to a greater person, is rightly called the font of the virtues. Abundant humility, though, nourishes the virtues, and superabundant humility guards and amplifies them. Humility is diversified in seven ways. For humility is [first of all] in the laying down of temporal possessions. Six other [modes of humility] follow: two in the voice, two in the body, and two in the heart.[11] Two in

---

[10] For the same division of humility into sufficient, abundant, and superabundant, see Bernard of Clairvaux, *Sententiae* (Sent) 1.37 (SBOp 6/2:19; CF 55:133). There Bernard gives the same explanations of each of these three kinds of humility, though in more abbreviated form. It should also be noted that the Latin text from *Est alia sufficiens* ["There is one that is sufficient"] through *et non praefert se etiam minori* ["and does not give preference to oneself even over a lesser person"] is also found virtually verbatim in Hermann of Rein, S 40.4 (CCCM 64:173). The text of Hermann contains an additional sentence, translated in brackets above: *Superabundans autem est illa, qua homo se subdit etiam minori.* The text of Ps-Bernard from the PL does not contain this sentence but has the instructions "[*suppl.* tertia definitio]." It is not clear which text was written first, nor the relation of either to Bernard of Clairvaux's *Sententiae*. See also William of Saint-Thierry, *Epistola (aurea) ad fratres de Monte Dei* (Ep frat) 240, ed. Paul Verdeyen, CCCM 88 (Turnhout: Brepols, 2003), 277; CF 12:89.

[11] A similar list of different "modes" of pride is found in Bernard of Clairvaux, *Sermones de diversis* 47 (Div) (SBOp 6/1:266–67; CF 68:284–85): *Est enim superbia cordis, superbia oris, superbia operis, superbia habitus. Superbia cordis est, quando homo in oculis suis magnus est . . . . Superbia oris vel linguae, quae et jactantia dicitur, est quando homo non solum magna de se sentit, sed etiam loquitur . . . . Superbia operis est, quando homo exteriori quadam superbia, ut magnus appareat, agit . . . . Superbia habitus est, quando homo, ut gloriosus videatur, pretiosis se ornat vestibus* ["There is the pride of heart, the pride of speech, the pride of

the voice, because humble people speak patiently against the word of impatience and humbly against the word of boasting.[12] Two in body, because there is both plainness in clothing and mortification in the flesh. Two in the heart, both because they place the common counsel before their own and because, their own will set aside, they subject themselves to the command of another.[13]

5. Humility is like a certain subterranean hollow in which the treasure of the virtues is most securely hidden, where neither the violence of robbers invades nor do *thieves break in and steal.** Humility, moreover, is an impenetrable shield by which we are spiritually protected and an unfailing sword striking from both sides. For outward humility profitably strikes outward enemies that they might repent, and inward humility powerfully strikes spiritual enemies, that they might do nothing or, better, be themselves undone. From this, humility of the heart is rightly called a wall against spiritual trials, and humility of the body a rampart against outward impediments.** Humility is

*Matt 6:20

*see Isa 26:1

---

work, and the pride of dress. Pride of heart is when a person is great in his own eyes . . . . Pride of speech or of the tongue, which is also called boasting, is when a person not only thinks but also speaks great things about himself . . . . Pride of work is when a person acts with a certain exterior pride, so as to appear great . . . . Pride of dress is when a man adorns himself with precious clothing in order to appear glorious"].

[12] See RB 7. These ways or modes of humility "in the voice" bear a close resemblance to the fourth, ninth, tenth, and eleventh steps of humility in the Rule, which counsel the patient acceptance of hardship, silence, restraint from laughter, and modesty in speech, respectively.

[13] See RB 7. These two ways of humility "in the heart" correspond to the second, third, and eighth steps of humility in the Rule. The second step counsels against loving one's own will and the satisfaction of one's own desires, the third step exhorts one to submit obediently to the superior, and the eighth step teaches one always to follow the common rule or the superior's example.

also called a tower of strength *against the enemy*,* be- *Lam 2:3
cause just as the tower in some city is the beauty and
bulwark of the city, so is humility the beauty and bulwark of the heart.

6. There is moreover a useless humility, by which
people even remove themselves from a task and hide
in silence, because they fear to become debased if by
chance something that their conscience dreads happens to them. There is also another humility that is
not edifying but destructive, as when people immod-
erately put themselves down by words or deeds at a
time or place that is not fitting, and also at times with
onlookers who are easily scandalized. There is also
the simulated humility of hypocrites, who put forth
in their form of life the appearance of humility, being
proud of the same displayed appearance,* and al- *see Matt 23:5,
25-28
though they are proud in the hidden recesses of the
heart, they wish to appear humble in the eyes of others, acting deceitfully, like a deceitful goldsmith who
sells a silver ring covered in gold as a gold ring.

7. It must be noted that one humility is simple and
not overthrown by the praises of human beings; another is enriched by virtues and yet was not honored
by human beings; another was honored by human
beings and yet was not enriched by virtues. Those are
said to have simple humility who are neither subject
to vices nor sustained by an abundance of virtues from
which they might take pride; nor do they reveal themselves to anyone in these things that they achieve. But
when humility is either honored or disdained by men
and women, it is grievously assaulted, because human
praise, even if not sought after, nevertheless delights
once offered,* and criticism, even if not feared when- *see Prov 27:21
ever it is absent, nevertheless wounds the unwary
when it comes.

8. But I consider what must not be overlooked, that
the virtue of humility among other virtues is called
excellent because the only Son of God especially exhibits this in himself as an example for us, and by this

*Ps 38:12; 64:5;
Prov 22:5

virtue all of the manifold snares of the enemy are
eluded.* For when Anthony saw all the snares of the
enemy spread out against him, and when with wonder he sought one able to escape them, the divine
voice responded to him thus: "Only humility."[14] But
whoever you are, if you accumulate the virtues without having humility, you are like one who carries dust
in the wind.[15] But if you wish to display the height of

*1 Tim 6:17

virtue, do not be haughty,* and then that which you
have done you will show to be more excellent. Do not
think that you have done anything when you have
acted, even all those things you have done most abundantly. Do not corrupt the fruits of your labors. Do not

*1 Cor 9:24;
Heb 12:1

run the course in vain,* lest you lose the reward of
your labor after completing a thousand laps. For if
you said that you should be praised, you have been
made culpable, even if you had been praiseworthy
before, but if you should confess yourself to be use-

*see Luke 17:10

less,* you have been made useful, even if before you
had been culpable.

[14] Also referenced in (Deacon) Pelagius, *Verba Seniorum. Bk.
15, De humilitate* (PL 73:953B–53C): *Dixit iterum abbas Antonius:
Vidi omnes laqueos inimici tensos in terra, et ingemiscens dixi: Quis
putas transiet istos? Et audivi vocem dicentem: Humilitas* [Again
Abbot Antonius said, "I looked at all the snares of the enemies
spread on the ground, and groaning I said: 'Who do you think
will cross these?' And I heard a voice saying, 'Humility' "].

[15] This section echoes Gregory the Great, Hom 7.4 (CCSL
141:52): *Qui enim sine humilitate virtutes congregat, in ventum
pulverem portat* ["For who gathers the virtues without humility
carries dust in the wind"]. The broader context of the quotation
is a homily on the fourth Sunday in Advent on John 1:19–28,
on John the Baptist's baptism of Jesus. In the gospel text Gregory
sees John commending humility to his readers. This dictum of
Gregory is also cited in isolation by others, e.g., Bonaventure
(*Commentarius in Euangelium sancti Lucae*, in Bonaventura, *Opera
omnia* [Ad Claras Aquas (Quaracci): Collegii S. Bonaventurae,
1895], 7:453; Robert Karris, trans., *Commentary on the Gospel of
Luke, Part III, Chapters 17–24* [New York: Franciscan Institute
Publications, 2001], chap. 18, v. 9, p. 99); and Thomas Aquinas,
Commentary on the Sentences, bk. 3, d. 33, q. 2.

9. Wherefore it is necessary to preserve humility if it is present, or to acquire it if it is absent, in order that you may diligently examine not your good traits, but rather your bad traits both hidden and public,[16] and that you may also attend not to the evil deeds but to the good deeds of others;* if whenever their good deeds do not appear in public, perhaps they are concealed in secret, because it is pious to assume [virtues in others].[17]* Thus humility is made useful, so that by casting yourself down you may raise another person.

*Matt 7:1

*Matt 6:1-8

By contrast, proud people attending to their own good deeds (if there are any) and not attending to their many evil deeds, and attending to the evil deeds of others rather than their good deeds, disparage others and exalt themselves. Therefore a certain forgetfulness of past virtues is necessary for us, because in that way

[16] The theme of coming to self-understanding plays a large role in Bernard's *Liber de gradibus humilitatis et superbiæ* (Hum), SBOp 3:13–59; *Steps of Humility and Pride*, trans. M. Ambrose Conway, CF 13 (Kalamazoo, MI: Cistercian Publications, 1989): "Humility is a virtue by which a man has a low opinion of himself because he knows himself well" (Hum 1.2 [SBOp 3:17; CF 13:30]).

[17] The theme of hidden virtue is one that recurs in the text and is related to 1 Cor 3:3 and Matt 6. Hidden virtue mirrors the seclusion of monastic life on an interior, personal scale, emphasizing the conformity of the being of virtuous people over the recognition and conformity of what they do. It is further exemplified by Christ, whose divinity was hidden within the humility of his human flesh. This theme is developed further in this treatise in the examplary virtue of John the Baptist explicitly hidden within the cave of humility (§12). See also, e.g., Bernard's commendation of "the hidden piety" of Alvisus, Abbot of Anchin (Ep 65.1 [SBOp 7:160]); see also the 11th-century *Vita Burchardi Episcopi* (PL 134:534), in which the bishop's mourners uncover secret tools of self-mortification and are brought to praise God all the more for the hidden and concealed piety of the bishop: *felices actus apud Deum ita tectos et absconsos* ["these blessed acts before God thus covered and hidden"].

I understand that we should never recall to mind[18] any of our virtues. The memory of virtues is, however, related to the simple praise of God, and it is not only not reprehensible, but praiseworthy.[19] Nevertheless, while your good works frequently attract the notice of people, beware lest someone tears them apart, because the Pharisee was practiced in speech, parading his own good works, and so the devil snatched them away.[20]* For blaming others to praise God is not thanksgiving but only the abandonment of virtues.

*Luke 18:9-14

10. Let us therefore avoid saying something boastfully about ourselves alone; this, indeed, makes us odious to both God and people. Therefore, as much as we have done good deeds, so little should we say about ourselves.* When we have done any holy deeds, we without a doubt hold God as debtor;[21] when we

*1 Cor 9:16;
see Rom 4:2

---

[18] *Meminerimus* from *memini, meminisse* (to remember, to recall to mind) is a deliberate play on the use of *oblivio* (forgetfulness) in the previous clause. However, the author seems to mean that one should not repeatedly remember one's virtuous acts, reliving them either by thinking about them or by telling others about them, and therefore congratulating oneself as opposed to progressing in the development of virtues.

[19] This sentence seems to qualify the previous sentence, putting to rest an objection. In general it is good to think on acts of virtue and virtuous persons as products of God's grace and thus indicative of God's glory worked through and in human beings. Inasmuch as remembering virtuous persons and their deeds is part of praising God, it is neither bad nor indifferent but good, but such praise is not the recalling against which the previous sentence warns, because it is thinking on these virtues and deeds under the aspect of God's activity of bringing them about rather than one's own.

[20] Bernard also uses the example of the Pharisee who exalted himself both by proclaiming his own good works and by pointing out others' faults (Hum 5.17 [SBOp 3:29; CF 13:45]).

[21] Here the author understands charitable deeds within an economic metaphor. For a detailed examination of *Deum debitorem*, see Gary A. Anderson, *Charity: The Place of the Poor in the Biblical Tradition* (New Haven: Yale University Press, 2013).

truly consider our works to be nothing, we merit more from such a disposition than on account of the deeds that we have done.[22] Thus the good of humility exceeds the merits of all the virtues. If humility is not present, the other virtues will not be able to be praiseworthy, but if humility is present, the other virtues with humility advance.[23] If we add the examples of the fathers, we will make clear what is better.

11. The centurion humbling his heart said to the Lord, *I am not worthy that you should enter under my roof,** and thereby he was made worthy. Indeed, as Paul said, *I am the least of the apostles, who am not worthy to be called an apostle,** and therefore he was found great before God and men. Thus even the woman who humbly bowed at the feet of the Lord was elevated by God

*Matt 8:8

*1 Cor 15.9

Anderson cites Prov 19:17 and Sir 29:1-20 as well as Basil's second sermon on Ps 14, §5, and Ephrem's hymn in praise of Abraham Kiddunaya. According to Anderson, through acts of charity (especially almsgiving), loans given to the needy who are unable to repay the debt are understood to place God, who acts as surety on behalf of the poor, in the debt of the creditor. Yet in the following sentence the author seems to challenge the strength of the economic metaphor, suggesting that the attitude of humility with respect to one's deeds is of greater merit than the deeds themselves, more meritorious and thereby receiving greater reward, than is the "debt-holder" who holds God to an accounting (in the manner of debt) of his or her specific deeds.

[22] See Augustine, S 158.2 (PL 38:863; *Sermones de novo testamento* [157–83], ed. Shari Boodts, CCSL 41Bb [Turnhout: Brepols, 2016], 24–25). This part of Augustine's sermon argues that God is only made a debtor to us because of God's own promises. Nothing that we can do or give can make God a debtor to us, because anything that we might give of all that we have that is good has come from ourselves but takes its origin from God.

[23] In this sentence the author seems to be suggesting not merely the unity of the virtues but a special dependence of the other virtues upon humility. It is not clear whether the sentence means to suggest that the other virtues will not be able to operate or that they will operate but that in the absence of humility such operation will not be laudable, even though continuing to be conformed to the good.

*Matt 26:6-13;
Mark 14:3-9;
Luke 7:37-39;
John 11:2; 12:3-8

a little later, so that she was allowed to anoint the Lord's head with oil* as if a herald of the resurrection of the Lord to the apostles, and by this she was an apostle to the apostles.[24] And also, while David danced naked before the ark of the Lord and was despised by Michal, the daughter of Saul, by putting forward the appearance of humility in dress David preserved the virtue of humility in his heart, as he makes known to us by his humble speech when he says, *I will play, and I will become more abject than I have done, and I will be humble in my own eyes.*[25]* But in this his humility appeared extraordinary, that although he was the mightiest soldier and future king, he did not esteem himself equal to a soldier but to a flea and a dog, not to the living but to the dead, since he spoke thus to King Saul: *Whom do you pursue, King of Israel? Whom do you pursue? A flea and a dead dog.** Therefore, by the merit of his humility, he was brought over from servitude to kingship.

*2 Sam 6:22

*1 Sam 24:15

Likewise the publican, praying in the temple and condemned by the Pharisee, when his conscience ac-

---

[24] This title *apostola apostolorum* for the woman who anointed Jesus, often conflated with Mary Magdalene and Mary of Bethany, seems to date back to Rabanus Maurus, *De Universo Libri XXII* 2.4.1 (PL 111:84), and is used by Innocent III (PL 217:830), Thomas Aquinas ("Super Euangelium Iohannis reportatio," in *Opuscula Theologica* 20.lec. 3, edited by R. Cai [Taurini-Romae: Marietti, 1975], 466), and others. Bernard's use of the title *apostolae apostolorum*, which distinguishes multiple Marys, may offer an interesting contrast with the use of *apostola apostolorum* here. See Katherine Ludwig Jansen, "Maria Magdalena: *Apostolorum Apostola*," in *Women Preachers and Prophets through Two Millennia of Christianity*, ed. Beverly Kienzle and Pamela J. Walker (Berkeley and Los Angeles: University of California Press, 1998), 57–96.

[25] This passage from 2 Samuel is used by Bernard on a similar point in a letter rebuking Oger, a canon regular of Mont-Saint-Eloi, for his resignation as superior of his monastery in order to return to the life of a monk (Bernard of Clairvaux, Ep 87.12 [SBOp 7:231]).

cused his heart did not dare to raise his eyes to heaven,[26] but striking his breast said, *O God, be merciful to me a sinner;** thus surely he came down from the temple more justified than the Pharisee.* And likewise Peter, since he was prince of the apostles,[27] was the most humble of all.[28] And thus he had such great merit before God that the sick were healed when the shadow of his body was cast over them.*

12. Thus also John the Baptist was announced by the angel* and filled with the Holy Spirit even from the womb of his mother,* and, though not yet born, perceived the advent of the Lord by the office of forerunner.[29] Then, already as a youth, he was a contemner

*Luke 18:13
*see Luke 18:14

*see Acts 5:15

*Luke 1:13
*Luke 1:41

---

[26] Bernard alludes to the publican's downcast eyes in *Steps of Humility and Pride* in the first step of pride (curiosity): "Dare you lift your eyes up to heaven, you who have sinned against heaven?" (Hum 10.28 [SBOp 3:38; CF 13:57]).

[27] This traditional title for the apostle Peter occurs, e.g., in Augustine, Jerome, Bernard, and Aelred of Rievaulx: Augustine, *In Johannes evangelium tractatus* 89.1 (CPL 278, 89, 31); Jerome, *Commentariorum in Esaiam libri XII–XVIII* 14.53.8; *Commentarii in prophetas minores: In Amos* 2.4, *In Zachariam* 2.10; *Dialogi contra Pelagianos* 1.23 (CCSL 73A:104; CCSL 76:319; CCSL 76A:188; CCSL 80); Bernard of Clairvaux, Div 4.5 [SBOp 6/1:97; CF 68:34]; *Sermones super Cantica Canticorum* [hereafter SC] 46.6 [SBOp 2:59; CF 7:245]); Aelred, SS 112:1, 10; 113.7; 135.2 (CCCM 2C:146, 148, 319, 416).

[28] This statement seems to deduce Peter's humility from his honored status among the apostles, perhaps on the basis of the logic of Luke 18:14—"everyone who exalts himself shall be humbled, and he who humbles himself shall be exalted"— which directly follows the verse just quoted (see Matt 19:30; 20:16). In addition, the gospels contain several episodes where Peter acts over confidently at first and learns humility by experience: see Matt 14:29-31; 16:21-23; 26:33-35, 69-75; Mark 8:31-33; 14:29-31, 66-72; Luke 22:33-34, 54-62; John 13:36-38; 18:15-18, 25-27; 21:15-19.

[29] This description of John the Baptist and the passage that follows from *annuntiatus per angelum* ["announced by the angel"] to *secundum vero spiritualem sensum sic exponitur* ["it is explained another way according to the spiritual sense"] is also found virtually verbatim in Hermann of Rein, S 40.4 (CCCM

*Matt 11:18;
Luke 1:80; 3:2

*Matt 3:4-6;
Mark 1:5-7

*Song 5:10
*John 1:30

*Phil 2:3

*John 1:20

*Luke 3:16

*Ps 108:10;
Ps 59:10

*Ps 59:10

of the world, an inhabitant of the desert,* uncultivated in appearance, remarkable through abstinence, an exceptional preacher, baptizer of the Lord,* *ruddy* by martyrdom, *white* by virginity. And *chosen out of thousands** to rank behind the Son of the Virgin and the Virgin Mother,* for that reason he was also judged by the people to be the Christ. I say, although he was of such like and measure, he chose to remain surely in himself, lest *through empty glory** he be carried away above himself. For *He confessed and did not deny it; he confessed: "I am not the Christ."** But because he humbly confessed the truth, he ascended to a still more perfect step of humility. For he said, *He who comes after me is greater than I, of whom I am not worthy to loosen the thongs of his sandals.** If these words are understood only literally, his humility would be pleasing enough.

However, it is explained in another way according to the spiritual sense. By the Lord's sandals, the incarnation of the Lord is understood,[30] as the Lord said through the psalmist: *Into Edom I will stretch forth my sandal,** that is, I will appear incarnate in the world, as indeed happened, and through this the foreign-born have been made subject to him.* But John confessed himself unworthy even of this, of loosening the thongs of the Lord's sandals, that is, of uncovering the mystery of his incarnation. In this his humility is believed to be so great that he placed himself under every

---

64:173) directly before the passage identified as shared material in §4 of this text. It is interrupted by a different explanation of the spiritual sense of the passage but is again close to verbatim in the final sentences of the paragraph: *Quia ergo inter natos mulierum . . . in foveam humilitatis abscondit thesaurum* ["Because there among those born of women . . . in the cave of humility"] (CCCM 64:173).

[30] This interpretation of the spiritual sense of the sandals is also found in the *Expositio in Matthaeum* of Rabanus Maurus Magnentius, ed. Bengt Löfstedt, CCCM 174 (Turnhout: Brepols, 2000), 48.

priest, whose office it is to uncover the mystery of the incarnation to others. Moreover, because among those born of women none is found more humble than John, therefore neither is there one who is greater.[‡] John has, therefore, safely hidden a manifold store of virtues[*] in the cave of humility.

‡Matt 11:11;
Luke 7:28
*see Matt 6:19-21

13. Thus also Mary, whom we call the "Star of the Sea,"[31] since she rose from a royal lineage, the form of

[31] The earliest attestation of this epithet seems to be Jerome's *Liber de nominibus hebraicis* (PL 23:771–858, esp. 789, 842), wherein he catalogues the Hebrew etymologies of names, including *Mariam, smyrna maris*, and *stella maris*. This etymology reappears in a couple of other early texts attributed with uncertainty to Jerome. Isidore of Seville follows Jerome, as does Bede in his work *In Lucae evangelium exposito* 1.27 (CCSL 120, ed. David Hurst [Turnhout: Brepols, 1960], 31): *Maria autem hebraice stella maris syriace uero domina uocatur* ["Moreover, Mary, the 'star of the sea' in Hebrew, is truly called 'lady' in Syriac"]; Bede also expounds its significance in his *Homeliarum evangelii libri II*, Hom. 3 (CPL 1367). Alcuin follows in his *Carmina* 109 (Alcuinus, *Carmina*, in *Poetae Latinae aevi Carolini*, ed. Ernst Dümmler, vol. 1 [Berlin: apud Weidmannos, 1881], 336). Sedulius Scottus discusses the epithet in the first chapter of *In euangelium Matthaei*, in *Sedulius Scottus: Kommentar zum Evangelium nach Matthäus*, ed. Bengt Löfstedt (Freiburg im Breisgau: Verlag Herder, 1989). Hrotsvitha of Gandersheim dramatizes a discussion of the epithet between characters Maria and Effrem in her play *Abraham* from her *Liber II*, in *Hrotsvithae Opera*, ed. Paulus von Winterfeld, SS rer. Germ. 34 (Berlin: apud Weidmannos, 1902), 148. Bernard famously uses the epithet in *In laudibus Virginis Matris*, *Homilia* 2.17 (SBOp 1:4), in his hymn *Ave Maris Stella*, as well as in a handful of sermons (see SBOp 1:4; 5:279); Aelred of Rievaulx makes heavier homiletic use of it and discusses its propriety in his Marian sermons 159 and 161–63 (CCCM 2C:488–511). Hildegard von Bingen uses and discusses it in several of her prose and poetic works, including *Scivias* (ed. Adelgundis Führkötter, 2 vols., CCCM 43A [Turnhout: Brepols, 1978], 860), several visions in her *Liber diuinorum operum* (ed. Albert Derolez and Peter Dronke, CCCM 226 [Turnhout: Brepols, 1996]), and as a refrain in her hymn *O Clarissima Mater*, *Carmen* 9 (in *Opera Minora*, ed. Hugh Feiss, et al., CCCM 226

all goodness, both Lady and Mother of Men, Queen of the Angels,[32] fruitful virgin of virgins,[33] was deified, having neither a prior nor subsequent likeness,[34] indeed the temple of the Lord,[35] the shrine of the Holy Spirit, whom the splendor of paternal glory elected.[36]

[Turnhout: Brepols, 2007], 371–477). Bonaventure quotes Bernard, implementing the epithet consistently in his lengthy meditation on the Virgin in S 39, *De purificatione b. Mariae Virginis* (*Sermons de diversis*, 2 vols., ed. Jacques Guy Bougerol [Paris: Editions Franciscaines, 1993], 2:527). In this sermon he expresses the epithet's pervasiveness: *Principalis interpretatio Mariae est stella maris et ista interpretatio omnes alias comprehendit* ["The principal interpretation of Mary is star of the sea, and this interpretation comprehends all others"].

[32] See Aelred of Rievaulx, S 153.6, *In assumptione sanctae Mariae* (CCCM 2C:441): *Quare hortatur ut surgat regina angelorum, domina mundi, mater eius qui mundat immundum iustificans impium?* ["How does one pray in order to raise up the queen of the angels, mistress of the world, mother of him who purified the impure, justifying the wicked?"]

[33] See Aelred of Rievaulx, S 167.7, *In assumptione sanctae Mariae* (CCCM 2C:528): *Sic sublimasti humilem, sic fecundasti uirginem, ut uirgo pariat Dei Filium, et humilis habeat sponsum Deum* ["Just as you have ascended in humility, as you have been fruitful in virginity, the virgin gave birth to the Son of God and the lowly one had God for a bridegroom"].

[34] See Sedulius, *Carmen Paschale* 2.67–68 (CPL 1447:48): *Gaudia matris habens cum virginitatis honore / Nec primam similem visa es nec habere sequentem* ["Having the joy of the mother with honor of virginity, / You are seen to have neither a first nor a subsequent likeness"]. Also see Rupert of Deutz, *Commentaria in Canticum canticorum* lib. 6 (CCCM 26:139): *nec inter angelos nec inter homines similem uel primam habet uel sequentem habitura est* ["neither among angels nor among human beings has there either been a first likeness, nor will there be subsequent likeness"].

[35] This epithet is the first line of Peter Damian's Carmina 40, in *Hymnus ad Sexta*, 125.

[36] This description of Mary's election, *quam splendor elegit paternae gloriae* ["whom the splendor of paternal glory chose"], is found in Paschasius Radbertus, *De assumptione sanctae Mariae uirginis*, ed. Albert Ripberger, CCCM 56 (Turnhout: Brepols, 1985), 868.

Since she was, I say, of such quality and so great, she did not exalt herself about her celestial gifts but exhibited humility to the archangel Gabriel. She even took care to exhibit this [humility] before men: while bearing the Lord and man in her womb, as if merely a young maiden, she humbly devoted the favor of her servitude to her kinswoman Elizabeth, a woman of advanced age, and although she was humble and a virgin, it was not her virginity but her humility that the Lord is said to have regarded.[37] *My spirit rejoiced, she says, in the Lord God my Savior, because he has regarded the humility of his handmaid.** O humility, through which a woman was made the Mother of God, through which God descended from heaven to earth, through which souls* were transferred from hell to heaven.[38] This is the ladder set before you by God, by which you ascend from earth to heaven.[39]* By this ladder our fathers ascended; by this ladder also it is necessary that we ascend; otherwise we will not ascend at all.

*Luke 1:47-48

*anima

*Gen 28:12;
John 1:51;
RB 7.2

[37] The pairing and relative evaluation of humility and virginity is found in Augustine, *De bono coniugali* and *De sancta virginitate* (*The Good of Marriage and Holy Virginity*), ed. and trans. P. G. Walsh, Oxford Early Christian Texts (Oxford: Clarendon Press, 2001).

[38] A probable reference to the harrowing of hell.

[39] This reference to the *scala* (ladder) is probably adopted from Jacob's ladder (Gen 28:12) as discussed in RB 7. Bernard refers to the ladder in his *Sermones in festo sancti Michaelis* (2.17). Alternatively or additionally, reference to the *scala* may be a reference to Johannes Climacus's *The Ladder of Divine Ascent*, trans. Colm Luibheid and Norman Russell, The Classics of Western Spirituality (Mahwah, NJ: Paulist Press, 1982). The likelihood of this allusion is made more probable by Climacus's assertion in §71 that "Mary perfects the Synagogue," i.e., she perfects the means of God's descent to earth as discussed here. This comment is made in the context of Climacus's own discussion of humility. According to Paul Lachance, Angelo Clareno (d. 1337) translated Climacus's *Ladder* from Greek into Latin. See Paul Lachance, Introduction, in *Angela of Foligno: Complete Works*, trans. Paul Lachance (Mahwah, NJ: Paulist Press, 1993), 9.

14. But it ought not to be omitted how the steps of humility are arranged in the Rule of Blessed Benedict. For he says that the first step of humility concerns fear [of God]; the second, not to love one's own will; the third, obedience; the fourth, patience in obedience; the fifth, to reveal thoughts to one's father;[40] the sixth, to be contented with all lowly and last things, and to judge oneself undeserving of all enjoined labor; the seventh, not only to pronounce with the tongue but to believe with the heart that one is lower and more worthless than all others; the eighth, to do nothing except what is established by the common rule of the monastery and the examples of the superiors; the ninth, to constrain the tongue to silence until questioned; the tenth, not to be quick to laugh; the eleventh, that if speaking one ought to speak mildly, humbly, and reasonably, with gravity, and with few words; the twelfth, that one should demonstrate the same humility not only by a humble heart but by the example of corresponding outer signs, in modest

RB 7   clothing and plainness of expression.[41]

15. Although humility may be diversified with many modes, as it seems to me, humility is one. It grows in many different ways according to its interior and exterior operations: just as when one and the same human being crosses from infancy to childhood, from childhood to young adulthood, and thence to old age through different stages, a human being is one, not many, and just as out of a single root of a tree proceeds a trunk, and branches proceed out of the trunk, and flowers and leaves proceed out of the branches, and

---

[40] One's spiritual father (abbot) is meant here.

[41] This list of the steps of humility follows chapter 7 of the RB closely, though the RB contains far more scriptural references and ends not with the exhortation to *vestium vilitate et vultus simplicitate* but with the monk's final goal, the perfect love of God. Bernard's *Hum* lists Benedict's twelve steps in inverse order, citing RB 7 in 2.3 (SBOp 3:18; CF 13:31).

thence fruits proceed, so good works proceed out of a single root of humility,[42] just like branches. So it is too with the state of poverty and devout words, just like flowers and leaves, and, next, the joy in the Holy Spirit, just like fruits of a good tree.* Therefore, if I rightly consider it, the virtue of humility is in the heart, the appearance of humility is in the mouth, the labor of humility is in the work, and the fruit of humility is here and at our arrival. Indeed God bestows grace upon grace,* because the Lord rests on the lowly and calm* even in the present, and by how much people have been more humble in this world, so all the more glorious will they be established in the kingdom.

*Matt 7:17-18; Luke 6:43

*John 1:16
*Isa 66:2

We said these things about humility on account of the novices, in order that they might understand humility to be the foundation on which it is right that the remaining virtues be established.

PART TWO:
On Obedience

16. Therefore, because obedience, like a sister, inseparably follows humility, let us speak to some extent concerning obedience. But the good of obedience is more clearly revealed through the evil of disobedience. For as disobedience arises in evil, so much does

---

[42] This image of a single root from which good works proceed as fruit is derived from the repeated biblical use of this metaphor and often linked with the idea that Jesus is the root of Jesse from which the good works of all Christians spring (Isa 11:1; Jer 17:7-8; Matt 3:10; 7:17-18; Luke 6:43). But the singularity of the root is more commonly associated with Christ and the virtue of charity than with the virtue of humility as it is here. See, e.g., Gregory, Homily 27.1 (CCSL 141:227–28; *Forty Gospel Homilies*, trans. Dom David Hurst, Hom 31, CS 123 [Kalamazoo, MI: Cistercian Publications, 1990], 212 [hereafter Hurst, trans., *Homilies*]), quoted in Thomas Aquinas, ST II-II, qq. 108.2, ad. 2.

*Jude 1:6;
1 Tim 3:6;
Isa 14:12

obedience arise in good. For disobedience embraces every evil. Disobedience made the devil from an angel,* it drove the first parents out of Paradise and afterwards handed over a countless number to hell, it empties good and multiplies evils, and it erects idols in the heart. The refusal to submit is the wickedness of idolatry. But of what kind and how terrible a sin is plainly assessed in the first parents. Thus to the one whom God placed in the Paradise of delights,[43] permitting to eat many and the best of different kinds of fruits,* God forbade only the tree of the knowledge of good and evil.* However, it is certain that that tree was not harmful as food; indeed, he who made all things exceedingly good had not planted anything evil in Paradise; "but so that the man, who was rightly created, might increase the better through the merit of obedience, it was right that, leaving one good behind, he should have been prohibited even from what was good, so that his conduct might be more truly virtue, both to the extent that he subjected himself to his Author that he might present himself more humbly,"[44] and that for him obedience itself might be the virtue by which he would please his Lord.

*Gen 2:8-9

*Gen 2:17

As truly as possible, I can say that the only virtue for every living, rational creature is to remain under the power of God, and that the first and greatest vice leading to ruin, namely, a person's wanting to draw on his own power, is named disobedience. He would not, therefore, have had any source to think upon and sense the Lord unless something had been com-

---

[43] The phrase "Paradise of delights" is discussed by Augustine in *De Genesi contra Manichaeos*, in *On Genesis*, translated by Roland J. Teske (Washington, DC: The Catholic University of America Press, 1990), 107–9, bk. 2, chap. 9.

[44] Gregory, *Moralia in Iob* 35.XIV.29, ed. Mark Adriaen (Turnhout: Brepols, 1979) (hereafter Moralia), CCSL 143B:1793–94.

manded to him.[45] "The tree of the knowledge of good and evil from which Adam was prohibited to eat indicates in us the mid-rank of the soul, that is, an ordered integrity.[46] This is said, as it were, to be the tree planted in the middle of Paradise and is called the tree of the knowledge of good and evil. For the soul ought *to stretch itself out to those things that are before,* that is,

---

[45] This passage ("that for him something . . . had been commanded to him") very closely follows Augustine, *The Literal Meaning of Genesis,* trans. John Hammond Taylor (Mahwah, NJ: Paulist Press, 1982), 2:41–42: "It was proper that man, placed in a state of dependence upon the Lord God, should be given some prohibition, so that obedience would be the virtue by which he would please his Lord. I can truthfully say that this is the only virtue of every rational creature who lives his life under God's rule, and that the fundamental and greatest vice is the overweening pride by which one wishes to have independence to his own ruin, and the name of this vice is disobedience. There would not, therefore, be any way for a man to realize and feel that he was subject to the Lord unless he was given some command." The Venerable Bede also makes reference to this passage in Augustine in his commentary on Genesis. See *Commentaries on the Beginning up to the Birth of Isaac and the Casting out of Ishmael* (*Commentarii in Principium Genesis usque ad Nativitatem Isaac et Ejectionem Ismaelis*), in *The Complete Works of Venerable Bede,* ed. J. A. Giles, vol. 7: *Commentaries on the Scriptures* (London: Whitaker and Co., 1844), 43–44.

[46] The term "mid-rank of the soul" (*anima medietas*) is used by Augustine. Roland Teske explains his use of the phrase: "In the Augustinian world there are three levels: God, soul, and body. God is utterly unchangeable, souls are changeable only in time, and bodies are changeable in both time and place. Hence souls occupy a mid-rank position beneath God and above bodies. The soul can turn away from God and turn toward itself and bodies, thus destroying the order in which it should stand" (*On Genesis,* 108 n. 60). The phrase also appears in Albert of Padua (1195–1231), *Most Beneficial Assemblies* (*Conciones utilissimae*), in his sermon on the twelfth Sunday after Pentecost (*Sermo duodecimae dominicae post Pentecosten*) (Paris, 1550), 302. There he writes, "The middle [*medietas*] of man lives after sin, but the middle soul [*anima medietas*] dies, namely the body."

*Phil 3:13

to God, and *to forget those things that are behind.** But if, however, forsaken by God, the soul is turned in on itself, desiring to enjoy its own power without God,[47] and has this sin as its consequent punishment, soon it will learn through experience what there is between the good that it abandoned and the evil by which it fell. It will have tasted this from the tree of the knowledge of good and evil."[48]

17. Moreover the sin of Adam was most grave, because *when he was in honor, he did not understand;** that is, although he was created to the *image and likeness of God,*[49]* he did not wish to remain obedient but listened rather to the voice of his wife than to that of God. And with the sin of the wicked angel and the punishment of that same sin having been perceived (to wit, that

*Ps 48:13, 21

*Gen 1:26

---

[47] In treating the first sin of the demons, Aquinas writes that the first sin was committed on account of a desire to attain ultimate perfection "by the power of his own nature . . . without God bestowing grace" (*De malo* q. 16, a. 3, co).

[48] This entire section is taken from Augustine, *On the Literal Interpretation of Genesis,* in Teske, *On Genesis,* 108: "But the tree of the knowledge of good and evil likewise signifies the midrank of the soul and its ordered integrity. For the tree is planted in the middle of Paradise, and it is called the tree of discernment of good and evil, because the soul ought to stretch itself out toward those things which are before, that is, to God and to forget those things which are behind, that is corporeal pleasures. But if the soul should abandon God and turn to itself and will to enjoy its own power as if without God, it swells up with pride, which is the beginning of every sin. When punishment has followed upon this sin, it will learn by experience the difference between the good which it abandoned and the evil into which it has fallen. This is what it will be for it to have tasted the fruit of the tree of the discernment of good and evil."

[49] On the *similitudinem Dei* (divine likeness) of Gen 1:26, see Augustine, *De Trinitate,* 14.16.22–19.26; William of Saint–Thierry, Ep frat, e.g. 200, 255, 271; 277, 286–87 (CCCM 88:270–71, 280, 284, 285, 287; CF 12:79–80, 93–94, 97–98, 99–100, 102); Thomas Aquinas, ST Ia, q. 93.

the devil was made from an angel), and with pride blinding his heart, he set up his throne facing the north wind, so that he might be like the Most High.* Indeed *his place had been made in peace, and his dwelling in Zion,* but because he willingly destroyed peace, he was forced unwillingly to experience manifold sorrows. Indeed, he *went down from Jerusalem to Jericho, and fell among robbers, who also stripped him, and having wounded him went away, leaving him half dead.**[50] For the one who has forsaken the vision of peace learned the evils of this world by experience.[51]

*see Isa 14:13-14

*Ps 76:3

*Luke 10:30

But the robbers, that is, the evil spirits, deprived him of the tunic of immortality. And indeed he was gravely wounded because he sinned gravely, but he was left half alive. Indeed, because he sinned, it was as if he died, and because he did not lose reason, it was as if life remained. For this reason, his sin was most grave, because neither necessity nor his own fragility nor ignorance of the good coerced him to sin. Ignorance did not coerce him, since there were not many restrictions on him, but one. And constantly

[50] This passage appears in another treatise falsely ascribed to Bernard, *Instructio sacerdotis seu tractatus de praecipuis mysteriis notrae*, Part 1, chap. 1, §2: "Having been exiled from the place of bliss, from the Paradise of delightfulness, you were finally thrust down into the valley of tears [Ps 83:7]; you became that miserable traveler, or rather that deviator, who went down from Jerusalem to Jericho and fell into the hands of mercenaries, into the judgment of malicious spirits, who, having wounded him in natural things, stripped him of graces as well, and left him half-dead and forsaken, afflicted by a double death of body and soul [Luke 10:30-37]" (above, p. 34).

[51] The phrase *vision of peace* occurs repeatedly in the sermons of Aelred of Rievaulx, most often in connection with Jerusalem. See for instance *Aelredi Rievallensis Sermones*, S 2.8, 4.8, 7.14, 34.10 (CCCM 2A:18, 38, 63; CCCM 2B:281; CF 58:79, 108, 146; CF 77:136).

seeing God face to face,[52] he was not able to lapse in memory. Nor did fragility coerce him, since he had free choice; he was not oppressed, as later, but was sustained by the illumination of the Holy Spirit and thus strengthened through the grace of God, so that he would not sin if he did not desire to do so.[53]

Nor did necessity coerce him, since he was not vexed by hunger, thirst, or any other misery. And if he, in anticipation of vexations of the passions, wanted to eat some fruit, there were a variety of fruits in Paradise from which he was allowed to partake freely. One of those fruits staved off hunger, another thirst, another the other passions.[54] Although he had all these nearby, nevertheless, as if they were forbidden, he

---

[52] This possibly refers to Gen 3:8. For other places in Scripture where one is said to speak with God face to face see Gen 32:30; Exod 33:11; and Deut 34:10.

[53] Augustine discusses the different states of humankind corresponding to his state before the Fall, after the Fall, in grace, and in glory. See Augustine, *On Rebuke and Grace*, trans. Robert Ernst Wallis, NPNF 5 (Buffalo: Christian Literature Co., 1886–1889), chap. 33; *On Nature and Grace*, chaps. 49–51, in *Four Anti-Pelagian Writings*, trans. John A. Mourant and William J. Collinge (Washington, DC: Catholic University of America Press, 1992), 64–67. This fourfold distinction becomes a staple in subsequent discussions on the states of humankind (i.e., the state of humankind before the Fall: able to sin and able not to sin [*posse peccare, posse non peccare*]; the state of humankind after the fall: able to sin, not able not to sin [*posse peccare, non posse non peccare*]; the state of humankind in grace: able to sin, able not to sin [*posse peccare, posse non peccare*]; the state of humankind in glory: able not to sin, not able to sin [*posse non peccare, non posse peccare*]) and occurs throughout scholastic literature. See Bernard of Clairvaux, *De gratia et libero arbitrio* (Gra) 7.21 (SBOp 3:181–82; CF 19:79); Peter Lombard, *Sentences,* book II dist. 25, a. 4.; Peter Abelard, *Sic et non,* q. 34; Alexander of Hales, *Summa theologica* lib. 3, I, inquis. 1, tract. 1, q. 1, cap. 1, num. 1; Thomas Aquinas, *Disputed Questions on Truth,* q. 22, a. 12.

[54] See Paul Gondreau, *The Passions of Christ's Soul in the Theology of St. Thomas Aquinas* (Scranton: University of Scranton Press, 2009).

strove for that very fruit from which he had been prohibited by voice of the Lord—as if it were enjoined upon him—so that he ate of that fruit. And for this reason he fell away from the Creator by free will alone, and all of his descendants were devoured by this curse, for he transgressed most gravely.

18. But this must also be noted, because as blessed Augustine testifies in his *Enchiridion*, in this sin many criminal sins are included. For because Adam knowingly elevated himself against God, there was great pride; because he desired what was more than sufficient for himself, there was greed. For greed is not only for material wealth, but also for exaltation. Because he hurled himself to death, there was murder; because by loving himself he alienated himself from the love of the heavenly bridegroom,[55] he committed the crime of adultery; because he usurped the prohibited food, there was theft; and because he did not believe in God, he committed sacrilege.[56] These and other similar things are found even now in us, when we knowingly act against obedience.

[55] The phrase "bridegroom of heaven" or "heavenly bridegroom" occurs throughout Aelred's sermons. See *Aelredi Rievallensis Sermones*, S 50.19 (CCCM 2B:32); SS 49.1; 104.1; 110.3; 154.6 (CCCM 2C:70, 97, 135, 455). It is also found throughout the works of Bernard of Clairvaux; see for instance SC 22.4; 27.7; 29.3 (SBOp 1:1, 131, 186–87, 204; CF 7:17, 79–80, 105).

[56] This is a paraphrase of Augustine, *Enchiridion*, NPNF 3, chap. 45: "However, even in that one sin . . . a number of distinct sins may be observed, if it be analyzed as it were into its separate elements. For there is in it pride, because man chose to be under his own dominion, rather than under the dominion of God; and blasphemy, because he did not believe God; and murder, for he brought death upon himself; and spiritual fornication, for the purity of the human soul was corrupted by the seducing blandishments of the serpent; and theft, for man turned to his own use the food he had been forbidden to touch; and avarice, for he had a craving for more than should have been sufficient for him; and whatever other sin can be discovered on careful reflection to be involved in this one admitted sin."

19. O, the dreadful evil of disobedience! For every person who acts contrary to obedience as it pertains to himself, while his own conscience accuses him, desires to be subjected neither to God nor to humankind but commits robbery, *grasping for the likeness of God.**Phil 2:6 Just as the will of God is unconquerable and subjected to none, so this one desires to be conquered by none and willingly subjected to none, since he is not subjected to God. Therefore, because he is unwilling to be subjected to God, and though he is surely unable to be God, he nevertheless wants to make himself equal to God, or even greater—and this is certainly evil. The former desire is certainly bad, the latter is worse, and both are most foolish.

But it is easy to consider how grave the sin of disobedience may be, not only in greater but also in smaller sins. For because Jonathan, still ignorant of his father's command, tasted a little honey on the day when all were forbidden to eat by Saul, divine grace was withdrawn by God in order that the victory on that occasion might be wholly suspended,[57] because the punishment that ensued from the sin was so grave that Jonathan would have died without objection, unless he had been liberated through the intercession of all of the people.* Furthermore, it is read that a certain prophet received a mandate from God not to eat until he returned from the place where he had been sent. However, another prophet came and said that God had appeared to him and that he revealed that he ought to eat, according to the Lord's commandment. Deceived by those words, the prophet believed and ate. And in what he believed himself to be obedient,

*Phil 2:6

*1 Sam 14:24-46

---

[57] Stephen of Bourbon (d. 1261), a Dominican friar in Paris around 1223, composed *Tractatus de diversis materiis praedicabilibus* (*A Treatise on Different Matters for Preaching*) in Lyon between 1250 and 1261. He treats both 1 Sam 14 (in *Tractatus* 3.5, CCCM 124B:182) and 1 Kgs 13:24 (in *Tractatus* 1.9, CCCM 124:363).

he was disobedient. Punishment followed such a fault of disobedience, with the result that a lion killed him on the journey. Nevertheless, the sin of disobedience was pardoned in death, as is shown through this: that the lion that had killed the prophet afterwards dared to touch neither the prophet's corpse nor his ass.[58]*   *1 Kgs 13:11-28
But if an offense is so gravely committed when the disobedience arises from ignorance, how much more horribly does one sin who scorns obedience when his conscience accuses him? Therefore, as was said before, it is evident through the evil of disobedience how great the good of obedience is.

20. But now let us simply describe obedience, briefly adding its divisions below: which things hinder obedience, which support it, and what its properties may be, and its dignity, perfection, and merit.[59] Now obedience

---

[58] See Gregory the Great, *Dialogues,* trans. Odo John Zimmerman, FC vol. 39 (Washington, DC: The Catholic University of America, 1959), 4:25: "The man of God, for instance, who was sent to Samaria stopped on the way for a meal, contrary to God's command. For this disobedience he was killed by a lion. But Scripture at once adds that the ass and the lion were standing by the dead prophet, and 'the lion had not eaten of the dead body.' From this passage we see that the sin of disobedience was atoned for by his death, because the lion attacked the living prophet and killed him, yet did not dare touch him once he was dead."

[59] The following definition of obedience as a virtue appears to come from multiple sources. Though we cannot be certain whether Ps-Bernard was a contemporary of Aquinas, much of his definition of obedience seems to reflect familiarity with the discussion of the virtues in ST II–II, q. 104, wherein Aquinas speaks of obedience as a moral virtue and as a "special virtue" when performed with the intention of fulfilling a precept that proceeds from another's (the superior's) will (q. 104, a. 2). A similar discussion may be found in Aquinas's *Scriptum Super Libros Sententiarum,* II, d. 44, q. 2, a. 1, ed. R. P. Mandonnet (Paris: Lethielleux, 1929). In both of these texts Aquinas makes multiple references to Gregory the Great's discussion of obedience in his *Moralia* bk. 35 (CCSL 43B), which Ps-Bernard also frequently cites (see nn. 6, 12–16, 20–22, 25). Later in this paragraph,

*animo

is a virtue by which a human being, his own will having been put aside,[60] comprehends in the mind* the things that are enjoined to be completed by work, unless opposed by an invincible cause or the authority of a superior forbidding the very thing that had been enjoined.[61] One obedience is perfect, another imperfect.[62] The imperfect is that which does not extend to the point of death. The perfect is that which is not consumed but consummated by death.[63]* Likewise,

*Phil 2:8

Ps-Bernard takes up a further theme from the *Summa* and from Gregory, on the way in which obedience proceeds from charity (q. 104, a. 3; see q. 105 on disobedience). On the other hand, Ps-Bernard may simply be elaborating upon monastic discussions of obedience. Bernard of Clairvaux defines obedience as a virtue and as meritorious in several of his works, explicitly in Div S 41 and implicitly throughout the *Steps of Humility and Pride* 3.6–7; 16.44; 18.44; 19.49 (Div 41: SBOp 6/1:243–54; CF 68:213–25; Hum: SBOp 3:20–22, 50, 52, 53; CF 13:34–36, 72, 74–75, 75).

[60] Hermann of Runa also speaks of putting aside one's own will (*propria voluntate postposita*) in two of his sermons, where the main theme is humility. *Sermones festivales,* 40, 86 (CCCM 64:173, 392). Ps-Bernard refers to the same passage from Hermann's sermon 40 in §4 of this work.

[61] In much of Ps-Bernard's subsequent discussion of the obedience owed by subjects to their superiors (which continues especially in §§27 and 28), we can hear echoes of Aquinas's discussion (ST II–II, q. 104, a. 4-6). However, Ps-Bernard would naturally have been thinking of the fifth and seventh chapters of The Rule of Saint Benedict, which enjoin full obedience to the superior (RB 1980, 186–89, 190–203).

[62] Though many authors speak of perfect obedience, including Bernard, who names Christ the "perfect example of obedience" in Hum 3.7 (SBOp 3:21–22; CF 13:36), and Aquinas in his *Super Sententiarum,* II, d. 44, q. 2, ad. 4, the description of "imperfect" obedience seems to be Ps-Bernard's own, interpreted from the biblical model of Christ and the disciples.

[63] Ps-Bernard is clearly thinking of Christ here, given the dichotomy between being "consumed" and being "consummated" through obedience to the point of death (Phil 2:8). However, he may also be thinking of the disciples' willingness to follow Christ in the face of persecution and death (see Mark

one obedience is of great merit, another of little merit, and a third of no merit, though it still seems to be obedience. The one of great merit is, according to what blessed Gregory explained, when "obedience has something from itself in adversities," that is, when it embraces adversities out of desire.[64] Obedience of little merit is when someone who is reluctant obeys in adversities. Obedience of no merit occurs in prosperities, when the obedient heart pants[65] for those same prosperities.

Moreover, one obedience is venal, another is servile, another is filial.[66] The venal is that which has regard for any kind of temporal convenience or for the glory of the world. The servile is that which is performed with any kind of fear that is not chaste. The filial is that which has regard for charity alone.[67] Filial obedience

---

13:12-13; Luke 21:16-19) and to live in a fashion that reflects Christ's death (see Phil 3:10-11).

[64] Gregory, *Moralia* 35.XIV.30 (CCSL 143B:1794). The following discussion of obedience in terms of prosperities is also similar to Gregory's *Moralia* 35.XIV.30–31, wherein he offers the examples of Moses and Paul. Ps-Bernard resumes this discussion in §23.

[65] Ps-Bernard may be comparing the "panting" (*anhelat*) of the heart after prosperities with the servant who instead "pants" (*respiravi*) after God's commandments in Psalm 118:131.

[66] Ps-Bernard's discussion of venal, servile, and filial obedience to some extent parallels Aquinas's discussion of the different types of fear. Aquinas distinguishes between servile, filial, and initial fear, the latter being a midpoint between the other two (ST II–II, q. 19, ad. 2). He further correlates filial and "chaste" fear (q. 19, a. 2, ad. 2). Hugh of St. Victor also references servile, worldly, initial, and filial fear in his *De Sacramentis* 2.13.5 (*Corpus Victorinum*, ed. Rainer Berndt [Aschendorff: Monasterii Westfalorum, 2008], 485). Finally, Bernard compares chaste or filial fear with servile fear in *On Loving God* (hereafter Dil) 14.38 (SBOp 3:152; CF 13:130).

[67] Filial obedience proceeds from charity just as filial fear proceeds from charity (Aquinas ST II-II, q. 104, a. 3), given that through filial fear God is called our Father and our spouse, again according to Aquinas (ST II–II, q. 19, a. 2, ad. 3).

is exceedingly good; servile obedience neither suffices for salvation nor is exceedingly evil; venal obedience is exceedingly evil, especially that by which one fraudulently strives to attain to the height of the office of superior, as when the one who as subject pretends signs of humility[68] but who as superior to others wickedly reveals horns of pride.[69]* Moreover, we owe the obedience of a subject first to God, then to superiors, and after that to one another: to God out of necessity; to superiors out of power, because we freely submitted our very selves to them; to one another, out of charity.

*see Ps 74:5-6

21. Further, obedience is for us a guide to the virtues, a guide to wisdom, to martyrdom, and to our homeland. I call it a guide to the virtues according to the saying of Gregory: "Obedience alone is that which sows the rest of the virtues in the mind* and protects those sown."[70] In another place, he says that obedience possesses the merit of faith, without which every un-

*menti

---

[68] In keeping with his frequent reference to Phil 2:6-8, Ps-Bernard contrasts those who "pretend" signs of humility with Christ, whose divinity does not pretend but demonstrates all true signs of humility by "being born in human likeness." Jerome speaks of Christ's demonstrating the "signs of humility" in this way in his *Commentary on the Gospel of Matthew* 4.28.2 (CCSL 77:279).

[69] The image of horns may connote either honor or dishonor, though Ps-Bernard clearly uses the image in the latter sense. Ps 74:5-6 declares that sinners who "lift up their horns" by acting wickedly will be judged by God. Alternatively, Exod 34:29-30 depicts Moses as "horned" (*cornutam*) after he speaks with God. The image recurs in Amos 6:12, where it illustrates Israel's pride and disobedience. See further Jerome's *Commentary on Amos* 3.6.12 (CCSL 76:308). The fact that the two peaks of the mitres of abbots and bishops were also understood to be horns may explain why Ps-Bernard draws on the image in his discussion of monastic superiors and the dichotomy between true and false humility. See further Ruth Mellinkoff, *The Horned Moses in Medieval Art and Thought* (Berkeley: University of California Press, 1970), 78–79, 94–106, 109–17, 121–22.

[70] Gregory, Moralia 35.XIV.28 (CCSL 143B:1792).

faithful person is found guilty, although he may appear to be faithful.[71] It is, moreover, a guide to wisdom according to this: "Have you desired wisdom? Keep the commandments."[72]* It is a guide to martyrdom, because whoever truly and perfectly desires to be obedient ought to endure the most burdensome sufferings* of the heart and body. It is a great consolation to us, however, because *if we suffer with him, we will reign with him*,* and because the consolations of God will gladden our souls according to *the multitude of our sorrows.**

    *Sir 1:33

    passiones

    *2 Tim 2:12

And just as the sons of Jonadab on account of the obedience that they showed to their father, namely that they would not drink wine and that they would remain in tents,* merited a blessing from the Lord,‡ so whoever shows perfect obedience to his superiors merits a blessing from the Lord, especially in three ways. The first is the blessing of virtues, according to that which the Psalmist says, *You will multiply virtue in my soul;** the second is that the soul departing from the body may immediately pass over to rest; and the third is that at the resurrection of the just, every son of obedience may receive a double garment,[73] according to that which is written, namely, *They shall receive double in their land.**

    *Ps 93:19; see 2 Cor 1:3-7

    *see Jer 35:5-10 ‡Jer 35:19

    *Ps 137:3

    *Isa 61:7

What is more, charity, simplicity, and harmony accompany true obedience, which is signified figuratively to us through this, that after Job recovered from his infirmity, each one of his friends offered him *one*

---

[71] Gregory, Moralia 35.XIV.28 (CCSL 143B:1793).

[72] This quotation is not the form found in the Vulgate, but Augustine uses it multiple times in his *Enarrationes in Psalmos* 118.8 (CSEL 95B) and his *Contra Faustum* 22.53 (CSEL 25:647). Ps-Bernard may also have taken this form of the verse from Gregory's Moralia 4.XXXI.61 (CCSL 143:205–6; CS 249:291).

[73] Gregory also speaks of the "double garment" of the saints, which corresponds to the glorification of both the body and the soul. Moralia 35.XIV.25 (CCSL 143B:1789). Gregory also uses the following verse from Isaiah 61 in the same section.

*Job 42:11
*see Prov 25:12

*gold earring and one sheep.** But what is signified by the earring, which is a golden ornament, if not obedience?* What is signified by the sheep, if not simplicity?[74] And why a golden earring, except because it signifies golden charity, without which obedience ought not to be! And why are one earring and one sheep recounted, if not because unity is joined by the bond of harmony

*see Phil 2:2;
Col 3:14

to charity and simplicity?* For such harmony ought to direct our every action, so that the scandal of division in the church does not occur by our imperfec-

*see Phil 2:2-3;
1 Cor 1:10

tion.*

*see Matt 6:24;
13:22; Mark 4:19;
Jas 4:1-4;
1 John 2:15-17
‡see John 12:25

22. What is more, love of the world and personal love vigorously impede obedience,* and obedience is vigorously strengthened if one despises the world and one's self.‡ These are the properties of obedience: the subject should obey—not anxiously, not lukewarmly, not with talk of unwillingness—but without hesita-

*see RB 5.1, 14-18

tion,[75]* and even to death. And this is the perfection of obedience, according to which perfection it is said,

*Phil 2:8

even to death.[76]* For one perseveres in obedience even to the abuse of words, another even to the loss of possessions; another even to the sufferings of the body,[77] another even to death, and only the last attains the

---

[74] The symbolism of the earring and the sheep that Job's friends give him comes from Gregory's Moralia 35.XIV.27 (CCSL 143B:1792). Gregory uses the term *innocentia*, whereas Ps-Bernard uses *simplicitas*.

[75] The Rule of Saint Benedict describes obedience without hesitation, reluctance, or grumbling as the first step of humility (RB 5.1).

[76] In Phil 2:25-30, Paul writes that he sends his brother Epaphroditus, who has been sick "even unto death" for the sake of Christ but was preserved by Christ to continue in his work. Christ also speaks these words before his crucifixion; see Matt 26:38; Mark 14:34.

[77] These are the three ways in which the devil tries our patience, according to Bernard in *Sententiae* (Sent) 3:53 (SBOp 6/2:95; CF 55:229–30). Hum 3.7 also argues from Phil 2:8 that we should be willing to suffer greatly for the sake of obedience (SBOp 3:21–22; CF 13:36).

perfection of obedience. It should also be noted that "we are commanded to maintain obedience even to death."[78]

Therefore, lest obedience even to the end of the present life appear laborious, our Redeemer was made obedient even to death. What wonder is it, therefore, if human beings, sinners, subject themselves briefly to obedience in this life, when even the one who rewards those who are obedient did not abandon obedience?[79] But the aforesaid must not be overlooked, that it was said to our first parents, *from every tree of paradise you shall eat; but the tree of knowledge of good and evil you shall not touch.** For it is necessary that whoever prohibits his subjects from any single good must grant to them many other goods, lest the mind* of obedience perish entirely, if, having been refused all goods, it starves. For when he prohibited them from one, he granted all other trees of Paradise to be eaten, in order that he might more easily restrain his creature, whom he did not wish to deprive of life, from one so as to allow all the rest more broadly.

23. But as it was said above,[80] one who is obedient ought to endure adversities not only because of the precept but also out of one's own desire; however, in prosperity those obeying ought to have nothing at all from themselves, as we are able to truly affirm if we bring Moses and Paul as examples. For when Moses was pasturing the sheep in the desert, he was called by the Lord through an angel speaking in the fire* and was commanded to take charge of the multitude of all the Israelites, but because humility was fixed in his

*Gen 2:16-17

*mens

*Exod 3:1-6

---

[78] The repetition that obedience to death is "commanded" parallels Gregory's Moralia 35.XIV.28 (CCSL 143B:1793).

[79] The two preceding sentences, from "Therefore" to "did not abandon obedience," closely parallel Gregory, Moralia 35.XIV.28 (CCSL 143B:1793).

[80] Presumably referring to the words of Gregory in ¶20 (see n. 64).

mente   heart, he immediately feared the glory of so great a
command offered to him and promptly hastened to
plead his weakness, saying, *I implore you, Lord, I have
never*[81] *been eloquent; from the time you began to speak to
*Exod 4:10   your servant, I was slow and constrained of tongue;** and
having thus placed himself, he earnestly requests that
*Exod 4:13   another go, saying, *Send whom you will send.** Behold,
when Moses speaks to the Creator of speech, lest he
receive the power of such governance, he pleads himself to be without eloquence.

However, Paul says, *I am ready not only to be impris-
*Acts 21:13   oned but even to die in Jerusalem for the name of Jesus,** for
*Acts 20:24   I do not account my life more precious than myself.** Therefore, proceeding to Jerusalem, he recognizes the
adversities and nevertheless cheerfully longs for this:
he hears of what he should fear but passionately pants
for this.[82] Moses, therefore, has nothing from himself
for the sake of prosperity, because he resists through
prayers lest he be put over the people of Israel; furthermore Paul is led towards adversities by his own wish,
because he gains knowledge of the imminent evils,
and yet his spirit burns with devotion toward bitter
adversities. Moses wished to avoid the glory of present
power though the Lord commanded him, and with
the Lord ordaining, Paul strove through hardships
and perils to hasten toward even heavier burdens.
Therefore we are profitably instructed by the example
of the preceding men, with the result that if we
struggle to truly grasp the palm of obedience, we fight
the prosperity of this world because of the command
alone, but we fight adversity out of devotion.[83]

---

[81] Literally, "from yesterday and the day before yesterday."

[82] Here Ps-Bernard returns to the comparison of those who
pant for prosperity and those who pant for adversity out of
obedience. See ¶20 n. 65.

[83] The majority of §23, beginning with the example of Moses,
is taken from Gregory's *Moralia* 35.XIV.31 (CCSL 143B:1795–96).
The same biblical passages are cited, and the Latin is nearly
identical, though Gregory also inserts Gal 2:1-2 concerning

24. It should also be noted how much may be gathered from human reason. Just as nothing evil ought to be enjoined from a precept by superiors, so not all goods, but moderate goods, ought to be enjoined,[84] which are given to us by the Lord as if out of our own power, for example, just as to read, to write, to speak, to be silent, to work, to stop, and similar things are given to us. But, just as it was said, not all goods ought to be commanded. For who would dare to enjoin someone through obedience to leave everything, to take up the vow of virginity, to abide in virginity, to love the enemy, to die for one's neighbor?* Yet if anyone has faith like the *mustard seed*,‡ that one is able and even obliged to embrace these things that seem impossible according to human reason, if they are enjoined by a superior. For many of the holy, transcending human reason by faith, have walked on water* and removed mountains from their places.‡

*Matt 5:44; see Luke 10:27-37
‡Matt 17:19; Mark 4:31; Luke 17:6

*Matt 14:25-31; Mark 6:48; John 6:19
‡Matt 17:19; Mark 11:23; 1 Cor 13:2

25. Now, what the dignity of obedience is remains to be shown. In truth, the dignity of obedience is most like God. For one who simply keeps charity in behavior has the likeness of God. However, one who with charity also vigilantly pursues fasts, vigils, and other labors of the virtues* is more like God. But one who, with all these things, binds the very self by the bond of obedience under the power of another and depends on the will and command of his master in all things, keeping obedience *even unto death*,* is most like God.[85]

*see 1 Cor 13:1-3; 2 Cor 6:5; 11:27

*Phil 2:8

Paul's trip to Jerusalem. The use of Moses and Paul as exemplars of obedience, as well as the very similar Latin phrasing of the last half of this paragraph, can also be found in a sermon of the lesser-known Ps-Augustinus Belgicus, which has been variously dated between the 12th and the 14th centuries (*Sermones ad fratres in eremo commorantes* 5; PL 40:1243).

[84] Moderation, or the middle way, is a common trope in medieval religious life. The Rule of Saint Benedict instructs that "all things are to be done with moderation on account of the fainthearted" (RB 48.9).

[85] One who achieves such a state of obedience is like Christ, who was "obedient even unto death" (Phil 2:8). Augustine too

However, the merit of obedience will be unto eternal life in the kingdom, and there all will be made more exalted the more perfect they remain in that same obedience here. And those especially merit to be exalted by God who preserve the virginity of obedience *even unto death.*

We are calling "virginity of obedience" the incorruption of obedience, namely, when those who from the moment[86] that they have subjected themselves to a master have not been disobedient at any hour, whether in act or in will. And just as in the kingdom of life all who remained virgins in flesh and spirit but did not preserve the virginity of obedience will sing a new song to the Lamb, but not the song of the virginity of obedience, so conversely all who remained in the virginity of obedience and did not preserve the virginity of the flesh and of the spirit, even if they will not sing the song of virgins, will nonetheless sing the song of the virginity of obedience before the Lord and the Lamb.[87]

---

connects likeness to God with obedience, arguing that one who loves one's enemies and prays for one's persecutors is like God (Matt 5:44-45). To do so is obedience. The story of the first humans in Paradise also demonstrates this connection. Adam and Eve sought to be like God in a perverse fashion and became like "foolish beasts." However, when they were under God's dominion and submissive to God's command, they were truly like him. Indeed the precept given to Adam and Eve, which forbade them to touch what was not evil in itself, demonstrates that "obedience alone wins the victory, and disobedience alone earns punishment." See Augustine, *Ennarationes*, 70.2.6–7; *Expositions of the Psalms 51–72*, trans. Maria Boulding, vol. III/17 (Hyde Park, NY: New City Press, 2001), 442–46.

[86] Taking *ex quo* as *ex quo (tempore)*.

[87] Talk of virgins singing a new song is taken from Rev 14:4. In the present passage, this is distinguished from a song to be sung by those who have preserved obedience without corruption. The "song of the virginity of obedience" would seem superior to the song of virgins, in the sense that those who keep obedience uncorrupted, even if not themselves virgins in flesh and spirit, are superior to those who are virgins in flesh and

26. Great, therefore, is the virtue of obedience, which in a certain way makes virgins out of those who have been corrupted. This virtue leads the soldiers of Christ[88] *through fire and water* that they might cross over *into refreshment.** It tests them and, having tested them, renders them perfect—perfect and therefore victors.[89]* For *the obedient man speaks of victories.*‡ Indeed,

*Ps 65:12

*see Jas 1:3-4, 12
‡Prov 21:28

---

spirit but are not themselves obedient. There are echoes in this passage of Augustine, *De bono coniugali* 29: "And there is this further, that people are not rightly compared with people in regard of some one good. For it may come to pass that one has not what another has but has another thing, which must be esteemed of more value. The good of obedience is better than that of continence. For marriage is in no place condemned by authority of our Scriptures, but disobedience is in no place acquitted. If therefore there be set before us a virgin about to continue so but yet disobedient, and a married woman who could not continue a virgin but yet obedient, which shall we call better? Shall it be (the one) less praiseworthy than if she were a virgin, or (the other) worthy of blame, even as she is a virgin? So, if you compare a drunken virgin with a sober married woman, who can doubt to pass the same sentence? Forsooth marriage and virginity are two goods, whereof the one is greater; but sobriety and drunkenness are, even as obedience and stubbornness, the one good and the other evil. But it is better to have all goods even in a less degree than great good with great evil, forasmuch as in the goods of the body also it is better to have the stature of Zaccheus with sound health than that of Goliath with fever" (*The Good of Marriage*, ed. Walsh).

[88] The term *milites Christi* occurs frequently. Although it is not found in Scripture, it may have roots in Eph 6:10-17, where Christians are encouraged to "put on the whole armor of God." It is also found in, e.g., Ambrose of Milan, Sulpicius Severus, Peter Damian, and Aelred of Rievaulx among others: see Ambrose, *De patriarchis* 11.56 (CPL 132:158); *Expositio evangelii secundum Lucam* 1 (CCSL 14); Sulpicius Severus, *De vita Beati Martini* 1.4 (PL 20:162D); Peter Damian, Ss 17.1, 2; 30.1; and 32.3 (PL 144:592D, 601A, 670C, and 676C); and Aelred of Rievaulx, S 124.34 (CCCM 2C:251).

[89] See the anonymous *Expositio super septem libri apocalypsis* 3.18 (PL 17:791C): "the tested and perfected receive everything that they are able to receive." The Patrologia Latina places this text with the works of Ambrose, but it is no longer thought to

*1 Sam 15:22;
see Eccl 4:17

whenever the obedient are enjoined to anything harsh or difficult, if they immolate themselves and sacrifice to God "by the sword of the precept,"[90] they speak of a great victory because they conquer themselves. For much *better is obedience than victims,** "because through the victim, the flesh of another is immolated, while through obedience the will itself is immolated."[91] The obedient person prays cheerfully and confidently, because as it is said by blessed Augustine, "Better is a single prayer of the obedient man than ten thousand of the one who disregards."[92] Obedience, indeed, directs toward heaven prayer, which without obedience does not ascend to the Lord, just as a stone thrown toward heaven does not touch it.

*Prov 28:1

The obedient person is confident like a lion.* And just as a lion does not trust[93] in the powers of others but in the powers of his own breast, nor does he tremble at the *approach* of some [other] beast, so also the obedient person does not glory in the prayer and life of others, but in his own conscience, according to these words of the apostle: *Our glory is this, the testimony of*

*2 Cor 1:12

*our conscience.** Nor is he fearful at the approach of evil beasts.[94] For if the "spirit of avarice" or "of pride" ap-

---

be his work. The text has also been attributed to the Benedictine Berengaudus (fl. ca. 859), but its authorship is uncertain.

[90] Gregory the Great, Moralia 35.XIV.28 (CCSL 143B:1792).

[91] Gregory the Great, Moralia 35.XIV.28 (CCSL 143B:1792). The segment of text from "For *the obedient man speaks of victories*" through "*the will itself is immolated*" is clearly based on Gregory's Moralia, although it is not quoted verbatim. Gregory quotes from 1 Sam 15:22 rather than Ecclesiastes.

[92] Augustine, *De opere monachorum* 17.20 (PL 40:565). The Latin word *contemptoris* is somewhat inelegantly translated here as "one who disregards" to underscore the contrast between the *contemptoris* and the obedient one. It might also be translated "despiser" or "contemner."

[93] The Latin word is *confidit*, translated "is confident" in the previous sentence.

[94] Gregory the Great, Moralia 31.XXVIII.55 (CCSL 143B:1590–91): "The lion, therefore, is not afraid on the approach of beasts, because he knows that he is stronger than all of them."

proaches him, or "of fornication" or any other evil spirit[95] who says, *Bow down, that we may go across,** the virtue of obedience itself invigorates him in such a way that he does not bow down but crosses over as a victor.[96] And no wonder! For the virtue of "obedience is the salvation of all the faithful, the mother of all the virtues."[97] Obedience is the discoverer of the kingdom of heaven;* obedience is what opens heaven and what lifts up human beings from the earth; it dwells with the angels, it is the food of all the saints, for by it the saints are weaned, and through it they come to perfection.[98]*

27. There are other ways that seem to pertain to obedience, although there is no truth of obedience in them. For there are those who choose an ignorant

*Isa 51:23

*see Matt 13:44

*see 1 Cor 3:2;
Heb 5:12-14

---

[95] Ambrose, *Expositio in psalmum 118*, 20.45 (CPL 141:467).

[96] The placement of the words of Isa 51:23 in the mouths of "unclean spirits" is found in Gregory the Great, Bernard of Clairvaux, and Aelred of Rievaulx: see Gregory, *Homilae in evangelia* 31.7 (CCSL 141:275; Hurst, trans., *Homilies*, 31.254); Bernard of Clairvaux, *Sermo de altitudine et bassitudine cordis* 1 (SBOp 5:214; CF 53:128), Div 40.4 (SBOp 6/1:237; CF 68:204); Aelred of Rievaulx, S 14.16 (CCCM 2A:118; CF 58:223–24); S 47.15 (CCCM 2B:7; CF 80); S 138.13 (CCCM 2C:345; CF 81). Aelred may be the most likely source here, given that he refers to both unclean spirits and spiritual beasts in SS 14 and 138.

[97] The precise term "mother of all the virtues" cannot be found in the texts of Gregory but appears to be derived from Gregory's claim that obedience "is the sole virtue that implants other virtues in the mind and keeps them safe when planted," which Ps-Bernard previously quoted in Pars Secunda, 21. This description of obedience is also found in Augustine, *City of God* 14.12: "However, what is really involved in God's prohibition is obedience, the virtue that is, so to speak, the mother and guardian of all the virtues of a rational creature" (see *City of God, Books 8–16*, Writings of Saint Augustine, Volume 7, trans. Gerald J. Walsh and Grace Monahan, FC 14 [Washington, DC: Catholic University of America Press, 1952], 379).

[98] The text from "obedience is the salvation" to the end of the paragraph is found virtually verbatim in Smaragdus of St. Michel's *Diadema monachorum* 13 (PL 102:610D).

teacher for themselves, not in order to obey such a teacher but in order to be able to bend him according to their own carnal will. Or they choose a learned teacher, who lives carnally and carnally loves those who comply. Therefore these who seem to obey in exterior things—not in order to please the Lord, but for the fostering of their own desires—are rightly called Ishmaelites.[99] For "Ishmaelite" means "obeying one's self."[100] And there is an obedience descending from excessive simplicity that we call "folly," when someone strives to obey the bad as much as the good, since it is written, "A sin should never be committed through obedience, but sometimes a good deed should be given up."[101] And there is the obedience that transgresses itself indiscreetly, when those deceived by excessive subtlety determine for themselves what superiors ought to enjoin and what they ought not.

And obedience has been destroyed when people choose in advance a good for themselves in order to request that it be enjoined on them by the superior (which is manifestly evil) but go to pieces through impatience when they are denied by the superior. But it is good if they remain unmoved when they suggest to the superior some good that they humbly desire and it is denied them. There is also an obedience, depraved by the pestilence of pride and simultaneously also of foolishness, that descends from one's own will, when people in the good works that they are going to

---

[99] While those who select a carnal teacher may appear to be keeping obedience, they fail to do so in truth because they have chosen a teacher who instead of challenging them to live spiritually teaches them to live carnally because of the teacher's love for flattery and imitation. According to Ps-Bernard, this is no obedience at all but rather a form of self-willfulness.

[100] This interpretation is found in Augustine, *Enarrationes* 82.7; *Expositions,* trans. Boulding; Bruno the Carthusian repeats it in *Expositio in Psalmos* 82 (PL 152:1078A), as does Peter Lombard, *Commentarium in Psalmos* 82.5 (CCCM 191:782).

[101] Gregory the Great, Moralia 35.XIV.29 (CCSL 143B:1793).

perform, if they be enjoined upon them, and which by no means. . . .[102] And whenever it happens that the superior never commands them [to perform] those goods that they do not want to do, nevertheless on account of their foolish deliberation and the disobedience of their heart* they are held *guilty of death*‡ before God.[103]

*see Ps 35:2
‡Matt 26:66

But also this must be known, that whenever a master enjoins something explicitly and the disciple in no way agrees but rather subjects the will of the master to his own will, as if he himself were the one giving better counsel (although he ought to bend his own will and counsel under the will and command of the master), he is led by deviant error far from the "way of obedience,"* since he thus makes himself master and his master his disciple.*

*RB 71:2
*see Matt 10:24;
Luke 6:40

28. Moreover it ought to be considered that subordinates should avoid the errors of the master in such a way that they always honor the master, because they are misled insofar as they imitate errors to honor the master, or insofar as they refuse to be subordinated to the master in order to avoid errors. Since while they

---

[102] Migne's text, marked by ellipses, is defective here. Given the following sentence, one might suppose this case: that the prideful and foolish one, who takes no delight in the good works he expects to be commanded to perform, intends rebellion if so commanded.

[103] This discussion of obedience in relation to the things that one desires for oneself resonates with Gregory's Moralia: "But because sometimes worldly advantages, and sometimes worldly losses, are enjoined on us, it should be especially understood that sometimes if obedience has something of its own, it is no obedience at all, but sometimes if it has not something of its own, it is a very paltry obedience. For when success in this world is enjoined, when a higher rank is commanded to be taken, he who obeys these commands makes void for himself the virtue of his obedience, if he is eager for these things with the longing of his own. For he guides not himself by the rule of obedience if he is eager for these things with longing of his own" (Gregory, Moralia, 35.XIV.30 [CCSL 143B:1794]).

*see Matt 7:3;
Luke 6:42

attend with careful subtlety to the acts or words of the master the nature of their own errors may lie hidden before him,* they are [therefore] ignorant of what lies hidden in themselves. And while they want to consider neither their great nor their small evil acts, but their good acts if there are any, they neither rightly perceive

*see Matt 6:4

the hidden acts* of the master nor approve his manifest good acts, but they gladly attend to the manifest evil acts, if there are any. And I say, while they do this, they idly elevate themselves, and, impelled by malice, they disparage the master.[104] Truly, attending to their own misdeeds, they confess that they are sinners.

Nevertheless, they do not judge that they have sinned so much that they ought to have been placed under such a teacher. With malice growing, they withdraw their word of reply, and they are more wicked in silence than they would have been in speaking.[105] But in this vice of disobedience, they are far from the

*1 Pet 1:14

*sons of obedience,** whose zeal is always to understand humbly, to think humbly, to obey humbly, and not to refuse the "habit of humility."[106]

We described simply these things about obedience and its purpose on account of the simple *sons of obedience*, but because charity is queen of humility and obedience, and all the virtues ought to be directed to her rule,[107] I wish, if I am able, to give drink to the new

---

[104] The word play on *extollit* (elevates) and *deprimit* (disparages or presses down) is lost in translation.

[105] In this extreme state of disobedience, disciples despise the master to such a degree that they no longer speak to him.

[106] This phrase is found in the Venerable Bede, *In primam partem Samuhelis libri iv. Nomina locorum* 1.2 (CPL 1346:698); Peter Lombard, *III Sent.* d. 36, c. 2, p. 4; and Thomas Aquinas, *Expositio super Isaiam ad litteram* 37.

[107] This notion of charity as queen and ruler of the other virtues has resonance with several other thinkers. Bernard of Clairvaux refers to charity as a queen in his *Parables*: see *Parabolae* 1.6 (SBOp 6/2:266). Richard of St. Victor calls charity the queen of the virtues: see *Mysticae Adnotationes in Psalmos* 44 (PL 196:321D):

brothers from the most abundant "font of charity." [108]
But because fear introduces charity, so entering with
the result that it departs, [109] let us propose some things
about fear.

_____

*Merito regina virtutum charitas esse dicitur, quia virtutis nomen
amittit quae charitati non famulatur* ["Truly charity is said to be
queen of the virtues, because the name of virtue dismisses what
does not serve charity"]. Alan of Lille calls charity both the
"form of the virtues" and the "queen of the virtues": see Alan
of Lille, *Dicta Alia* (PL 210:262B). For Thomas Aquinas, charity
is the "form of the virtues" because it directs the acts of all the
other virtues to God as end. He also calls charity the "mother
of the other virtues, because, by commanding them, it conceives
the acts of the other virtues, by the desire of the last end": see
ST II–II, q. 23, a. 8. In addition, Catherine of Siena brings together the three virtues of charity, humility, and obedience,
along with patience (*Dialogue*, trans. Algar Thorold [London:
Kegan Paul, Trench, Trübner, and Co., 1907], 166): "Wherefore
charity, the mother of patience, has given her as a sister to obedience, and so closely united them together that one cannot be
lost without the other. Either you have them both or you have
neither. This virtue has a nurse who feeds her, that is, true humility; therefore a soul is obedient in proportion to her humility and humble in proportion to her obedience. This humility
is the foster-mother and nurse of charity, and with the same
milk she feeds the virtue of obedience."

[108] Augustine uses the image of the "font of charity" to compare the unity of the Trinity in love with the unity that love
brings to the church: see *Tractates on John* 39.5 (CPL 278:24). Pope
Leo the Great uses this term to describe the charity that welled
up in Peter upon seeing Christ on the cross and washed away
the words of denial he had uttered in fear: see *Tractatus septem
et nonaginta* 60 (CCSL 138A:103). Leo's treatise is quoted by
Thomas Aquinas: see ST II–II, q. 24, a. 12, obj. 2. This term is
also found in Aelred of Rievaulx: see S 71.34 (CCCM 2B:230).

[109] Augustine argues that fear "prepares a place for charity."
However, once charity enters in, fear is cast out, for as charity
increases, fear decreases. Without fear, however, "there is no
way for charity to enter" [*Si autem nullus timor, non est qua intret
charitas*]. He compares this process to sewing: the needle must
enter before the thread, but the needle does not remain. Likewise, fear "enters only in order to introduce charity" [*intravit,
ut introduceret charitatem*]: see *Homilies on the First Epistle of John*

PART THREE:
Concerning Fear and Charity

29. Some fear is natural, common to us with the animals, proceeding according to the nature of the flesh. Indeed, we fear those things that are harmful to bodies, and naturally we avoid them, and we desire healthy things, wherefore it is written, *No one ever hated his own flesh, but nourishes and cherishes it.** This fear is not a sin, but punishment for sin; it neither introduces charity, nor does it expel it once it has been introduced, but this fear is in us naturally, whether we have charity or not. And Christ had this fear when he said, *My soul** is *sorrowful even to death‡* in order to show us by this the truth of the humanity he assumed,[110] and in order to strengthen by his example his own elect about to suffer adversities of the world and death. And no one should wonder at the elect one being shaken by fear, since Christ was sorrowful even to death.

30. But also fear, which is the beginning of wisdom* and is called servile, is believed to have been in Christ, about whom Isaiah says, *And he filled him with the spirit of the fear of the Lord.** Whence it is rightly sought how perfect charity and servile fear could be in him at the same time, since it would be sinful to deny that *perfect charity*, which *casts out fear,** was in Christ. Diverse things are said in answer to this; I do not know if they are adequate. It is said that he who received the other defects of our mortality[111] without any compulsion willingly had this too, since it is the gift of the Holy

*Eph 5:29

*anima
‡Matt 26:38

*Prov 1:7; 9:10;
Ps 110:10;
Sir 1:14

*Isa 11:3

*1 John 4:18

9.4 (PL 35:2048). Thomas Aquinas quotes Augustine on this point: see ST II–II, q. 24, a. 2, ad 3; q. 19, a. 6, obj. 1; q. 19, a. 8, ad 1; q. 19, a. 10, obj. 1.

[110] On *assumpti hominis*, see Augustine, *City of God* 11.2; and Peter Lombard, *Sentences*, III.6.

[111] On the defects of body and soul assumed by Christ see Thomas Aquinas, ST IIIa, qq. 14–15, and on fear in particular see q. 15, a. 7.

Spirit.[112] Nevertheless, perfect charity was in him. He had one from his perfection, the other from our infirmity. In other words, when it is said that he feared, it is understood that he neglected nothing, and the cause is put in place of the effect. For fear is the cause of this effect: that nothing is neglected.[113]

This interpretation seems to agree with the words of blessed Gregory, for he says the following: "To fear God is to omit nothing that should be done."[114]* Alternatively, it is said that Christ truly fears, but as he is in himself incomprehensible, so too he has an incomprehensible fear. Or it is said that Christ, who had knowledge of all hellish torments through his divinity, feared out of his humanity and felt horror within himself when he regarded those who were being tortured and were yet to be tortured, just as if one of us were to see someone else condemned to suffer extreme pains, that one would immediately begin to tremble in bodily complaint. Alternatively, according to Jerome, Christ had fear not for fearing, but for giving, even as a healthy doctor has medicine not for healing himself, since he is well, but for healing the sick.[115]

*Eccl 7:19

---

[112] The gifts of the Holy Spirit are enumerated in Isa 11:2-3. On the gift of fear see, e.g., Hugh of St. Victor, *De Sacramentis*, 2.13.5, found in *On the Sacraments of the Christian Faith*, trans. Roy Deferrari (Cambridge, MA: Medieval Academy of America, 1951), 377–81. Also see Peter Lombard, *Sentences* 3.34, and Thomas Aquinas, ST IIa IIae, q. 19.

[113] This argument is based on Eccl 7:19, "He who fears God neglects nothing" (*qui Deum timet nihil neglegit*).

[114] Gregory the Great, Moralia 1.III.3 (CCSL 143:26; CS 249:79). Job 1:1 says of Job, *Erat vir ille simplex et rectus ac timens Deum et recedens a malo* ["That man was blameless and upright, one who feared God and turned away from sin"]. A type of Christ, Job, *timens Deum*, possessed a fear of God that enabled medieval theologians to understand Christ's *timor Dei* by comparison. Commenting on Job.1:1, Gregory the Great cites Eccl 7:19: *Qui Deum timet nihil neglegit* ["He who fears God neglects nothing"].

[115] This elusive phrase may be a loose derivation of a gloss for Mark 14:33 attributed to Jerome in the *Glossa Ordinaria*: "*Pauere*

*animi

31. Diverse fears also arise in human beings. There is a fear that descends from vice of the soul* when people, lest they fail to gain temporal things or lose those gained, fear human beings more than God. This fear does not introduce charity but fights against any charity that has been introduced. There is also blameworthy fear when a person fears being cheapened, not in the sight of God (which must be feared), but in the sight of human beings (which must not be feared). And there is reprehensible fear when death itself and the passions of the body are feared beyond measure; thus the Lord prayed three times[116] that we might not succumb through the triple temptation of fear. There is likewise wicked fear, mindful only of hell, when a person fears neither God nor sinning, but burning. He removes himself, for the moment, from the sinful act—but not from the evil desire, because he would want to sin if he were permitted to do so without punishment. He does not love justice; he hates it. This fear is not called fear of the Lord, nor of correction, nor the beginning of wisdom.

---

et tristari docemur ante iudicium mortis, qui non possumus per nos dicere nisi per illud: Venit princeps huius mundi et in me non habet quidquam [John 14:30]" ["We are taught to fear and dread before the judgment of death—we who are not able to say on our own, 'the prince of this world is coming, and he has no hold on me' except through this"]. There is also a gloss attributed to Jerome of Matt 26:37 that addresses the reason for Christ's fear: *Christus timet quia ut Deus in corpore constitutus fragilitatem carnis exponit, qui corpus suscepit omnia debuit subire quae corporis sunt* ["Christ fears because, having been constituted as God in flesh, he exhibits the fragility of the body—he who takes up a body must undergo all things that are of the body"]. Kevin Madigan discusses Jerome's (as well as others') thoughts on Christ's ability to fear and suffer in *The Passions of Christ in Medieval Thought: An Essay on Christological Development* (Oxford: Oxford University Press, 2007), 64–72.

[116] See Peter Lombard, *Sentences* 3.34.

32. There is also a fear that has respect for God, namely, when we fear the Lord because of his power, since he is able to send the soul* and the body into hell. But the Lord commanded us to have this, saying, *Do not fear those who kill the body, but are not able to kill the soul;* rather, fear him who can destroy both the body and the soul in hell.* In this fear there is a little of the force of charity, in that it regards the Lord and is a gift of God, but since it stems from his power, it contains punishment and is called servile. In its beginning it is good, though it is not perfect; nor is it sufficient for salvation. Nevertheless, it becomes better by increasing degrees and heals one to the extent that one is not disposed to sin either by act or by will, even if bound by invincible sins. And this is called the fear of the Lord, it is called the fear of correction, it is called the fear of wisdom.

*animam

*animam
*Matt 10:28

From this fear, when the virtues mediate, we tend toward that fear that is said to endure forever.* And it should be noted that, for instance, a wife has chaste fear: that is to say, she fears lest her husband separate from her, or lest she offend her husband in some way. Thus the fear of the Lord is called chaste when people fear lest they offend God, from which one might lose the grace that one has received. And this fear, although it is the chaste sort, does not endure forever, since in the blessed life everyone is certain neither to wish nor to be able to offend God. However, the chaste fear that does endure forever, if it is considered attentively, may be called love.[117]* We love someone because of that

*Ps 18:10

*amor

---

[117] See Augustine's *De Civitate Dei* 21.24 (ed. Bernard Dombart and Alphonse Kalb, CCSL 48 [Turnhout: Brepols, 1955], 789–90): "It is, therefore, for those who hope in him that he makes his sweetness perfect, inspiring them with his own love, so that with a holy fear [*timore casto*], which love does not cast out, but which remains for ever and ever . . ." (*The City of God against the Pagans,* ed. and trans. R. W. Dyson [Cambridge: Cambridge

person himself; not looking out for punishment but rather gazing at that person, desiring him above all, we cleave to him chastely, and that chaste affection casts out fear. This is not customarily perceived from charity, which is had in the present, but rather from *1 John 4:18* that perfected charity that will be had in the future.* Then also fear is truly cast out, but it is expelled in the present through charity. For although fear is natural for humans, yet with the advent of charity, one is no longer enslaved because of fear, as before, but for God *Rom 8:15* himself.*

33. But Scripture commends the fear of the Lord in many ways. For example, it is written, *And with him who fears the Lord it will be well in the end, and in the day* *Sir 1:13* *of his death he will be blessed,** and, *the fear of the Lord is a* *Sir 1:22* *crown of wisdom, filling up peace and the fruit of salvation,** *Sir 1:25* and, *the fear of the Lord is the root of wisdom,** and, *the* *Sir 1:11* *fear of the Lord is both gladness and a crown of joy,** and, *Sir 1:12* *the fear of the Lord will give joy in length of days,** and, *the fear of the Lord drives out* and restrains vice, makes men and women careful and solicitous, *for whoever is without fear will not be able to be justified,* because where *Sir 1:27-28* there is no fear, there is the dissolution of life.[118]*

And elsewhere it is written, *Those who fear the Lord* *Sir 2:20* *will prepare their hearts,** and, *fear the Lord[119] with fear,* *Ps 2:11* *and rejoice in him with trembling,** and, *Blessed is the man* *mentis* *who is always fearful; but the one who is hardened in mind**

University Press, 1998], 1089). Among countless other examples of *timor castus,* also see Bernard of Clairvaux, *Sententiae* 3.92, trans. Maureen O'Brien, in *Bernard of Clairvaux: The Parables and the Sentences,* CF 55 (Kalamazoo, MI: Cistercian Publications, 2000), 142.

[118] What is not quoted from Sirach is taken directly from Isidore of Seville, *Synonyma de Lamentatione Animae Peccatricis* 2.26; see *Isidore of Seville's Synonyms (Lamentations of a Sinful Soul) and Differences,* trans. Priscilla Throop (Charlotte: MedievalMS, 2012).

[119] Migne has inserted here, "[fort, *servite Domino*]" (*fort* abbreviating *forsitan*).

will *fall into evil,** and, *Fear the Lord, all you his saints,*   *Prov 28:14
because those who fear him have no want,** and, *You who*   *Ps 33:10
fear the Lord, wait for his mercy, and do not turn away from
him, lest you fall,** and, *You who fear the Lord, love him,*   *Sir 2:7
and your hearts will be enlightened,** and, *You who fear the*   *Sir 2:10
Lord, hope in him, and mercy will come to you in joy,** and,*   *Sir 2:9
*You who fear God, believe in him, and your reward will not
be negated,** and, *Evil things will not happen to him who*   *Sir 2:8
fears the Lord, but in temptation the Lord will preserve him
from evils,** and, *The spirit of those who fear God is sought*   *Sir 33:1
and will be blessed in his sight,** and, *He who fears the*   *Sir 34:14
Lord will tremble at nothing and will not be afraid, because
the Lord is his hope, and power and strength lifted up his
heart.*[120]*   *Sir 34:16; 40:26

On this fear, Ambrose says, "Whoever fears the Lord avoids error and directs his ways toward the narrow path of virtue."[121] Gregory says, "If the crooked mind* is not first subverted by fear, it is not corrected   *mens
from its habitual faults."[122] But among these things it ought to be noted that the surpassing grace of God sends us a threefold thought, which concerns our deaths, the future Judgment of God, and the fire of hell. This opportune thought rouses the mind* from   *mentem

[120] The last clause of this phrase is oddly recontextualized, and since the unadulterated verse would appeal to Ps-Bernard's message, scribal error seems likely; Sir 40:26 actually says, "Power and strength lift up the heart, but above these is the fear of the Lord."

[121] Ambrose of Milan, *Hexaemeron* 1.4.12; in *Hexameron, Paradise, Cain and Abel,* translated by John J. Savage, FC 42 (Washington, DC: Catholic University of America Press, 1961), 12: "There is also the beginning of good instruction, as it is said, 'The fear of the Lord is the beginning of wisdom,' since he who fears the Lord departs from error and directs his ways to the path of virtue. Except a man fear the Lord, he is unable to renounce sin."

[122] Gregory the Great, Homily 34.6 (CCSL 141:304; Hurst, trans., *Homilies,* 285).

its own insolence[123] and leads us to fear, but the fear leads us to charity.

These things have been said incidentally about grace and the fear of charity. Concerning this charity, may charity herself teach us what is to be discerned, what is to be discovered, and what may be its beginning, its increase, and its perfection.

34. Therefore, let us assert that charity is spoken of in many different ways. For it is understood as a work of charity, as when it is customarily said, "charity is giving alms." That is a kind of charity, that when it does not proceed from the affection of the mind does not save. Charity also signifies God himself, as when it is said, *God is charity.** Also, charity signifies the purified affection of the mind, whence Saint Augustine posits such a description: "Charity is a movement of the soul to love oneself and the neighbor on account of God." [124] And it must be observed that when it is said that "Charity is a movement of the soul," the movement of the body is not essential, which, although sometimes that movement is a work of charity, nevertheless charity is not a movement of the body. And because the soul is moved to judge, and to similar things, it is said in addition, "to love," but because the soul is moved to love the world, it is said in addition, "God." Lest anyone hope for another reward from the Lord than God himself, rightly "on account of God" is added, and likewise, because no one ought to love

*1 John 4:16

---

[123] We lose a bit of the wordplay here; the Latin reads *opportuna importunitate*, emphasizing that the thought of hell is both suitable and unsuitable, or seasonable and unseasonable, and may recall 2 Tim 4:2.

[124] Ps-Bernard draws his quotation from the work *De Caritate*, an anonymous twelfth-century medieval treatise that slightly altered the original Augustinian version. Medieval theologians such as Abelard frequently used the version of the line cited by Ps-Bernard. For the original, see Augustine, *De doctrina Christiana* 3.10, ed. Joseph Martin, CCSL 32 (Turnhout: Brepols, 1962), 87.

oneself on account of oneself nor the neighbor on account of the neighbor, but on account of God, it is fittingly added, "and oneself and the neighbor on account of God."

And pay attention to how it has been rightly concluded "on account of God." People do not exist through themselves, nor are they good through themselves, but they exist from God and are good by God. I speak similarly concerning an angel and concerning any creature. For God exists through himself, and by him good is in him who exists through himself, and through him the good end of our beatitude is constituted: and therefore in God. But if people were to love themselves on account of themselves, or the neighbor on account of the neighbor, they would constitute the end of their beatitude no longer in God but in the creature, which is sin, where beyond doubt the person falls into misery, since no one is able to be beatitude for oneself, nor is anyone able to be beatitude except God. Therefore all ought to love themselves not on account of themselves, but on account of God.[125]

---

[125] See Augustine, *De Doctrina Christiana* 1.22.20 (CCSL 32.17; *On Christian Doctrine*, trans. D. W. Robertson, Jr. [Indianapolis, IN: Bobbs-Merrill, 1958], 18–19) on Augustine's distinction between loving the object for itself and loving it on account of something else. In this section Augustine defends the idea that God is the sole object of enjoyment (where enjoyment is that love that is a love on account of the object itself). In this passage Augustine interprets the Golden Rule, commanding love of neighbor, according to the first great commandment. Not only are we to love the neighbor as we love ourselves, but we are to love ourselves by understanding our own flourishing as the full occupation of the self (the heart, mind, and soul) with the love of God. To love the neighbor properly, therefore, is to love the neighbor's love of God and to desire the neighbor's love of God as the highest expression of the neighbor's being. The distinction between use and enjoyment, as well as the understanding of how the love of creatures stands in relation to the love of God, is extensively developed in later writers. See esp. Peter Lombard's *Sentences*, bk. 1, d. 1, c. 2, n. 4, which takes up

*Matt 22:39

*affectum

35. But because this charity cannot be shown or perfected unless it is confirmed by works—for "the proof of love is the exhibition of the work"[126]—it is necessary to attend to works that are exhibited for the sake of God. Thus it is said, *Love your neighbor as yourself**—for the sake of God, of course—that is, the service of God is to be fulfilled by that one. And this *as* here signifies similitude, not quantity. But just as you love *yourself* for the purpose of serving God, in the same way *love your neighbor* so that the neighbor might serve God and reign with God. For I dare not judge it a sin if someone has less affection* for another than for one's own self, but if the affection [regarding another] is equal [to that regarding oneself], it is perfect.[127] Moreover, we ought to impart corporeal and spiritual goods to these neighbors:[128] spiritual, such as prayers and

---

the question of the enjoyment of God and moral creatures in the discussion of the proper attitude towards theology (as a means to approach the enjoyment of God). For further discussion of Augustine and Peter Lombard's influence on this discussion, see Severin Valentinov Kitanov, *Beatific Enjoyment in Medieval Scholastic Debates: The Complex Legacy of Saint Augustine and Peter Lombard* (Lanham, MD: Lexington Books, 2014).

[126] Gregory the Great, Hom 30.1 (CCSL 141:256; Hurst, trans., *Homilies,* 236). This phrase is widely repeated in several medieval works: see, e.g., Aelred of Rievaulx, S 77.26, *In festivitate omnium sanctorum* (CCCM 2B:301); Albertus Magnus, *Commentarii in II Sententiarum,* d. 41C, a. 1 (*Opera Omnia,* 27:641); Bernard of Clairvaux, *Sententiae* 113 (SBOp 6/2:196; CF 55:373).

[127] It is customary in discussing love and loving to distinguish between what is willed and the mode of willing. *Affection (affectus)* has to do with the latter. The beginning of this sentence indicates a debate: is an affection that is lesser in the love of one person than the affection in the love of another a sin? The author leaves that issue open, while indicating that an equal affection for all is a perfect affection.

[128] The author is referring to a love of beneficence, which has to do with doing good, extending good, to others. He implicitly contrasts this love and a love of benevolence, which is to will good (in particular, the good of eternal salvation) to all equally, as beings made by and for God.

whatever befits the spirit, and corporeal, whatever we have beyond our need. We ought not to give to neighbors our goods in a time of necessity: we ought not to give but ought to share what is needed out of what we have. For thus Saint Gregory testifies: "someone is guilty as charged of loving the neighbor less who, although necessity urges, does not share necessary things."[129] And truly charity prefers that two people be afflicted by a tolerable want rather than that one person be tormented by an intolerable misery; nor is it wondrous, because charity, *which seeks not its own,** occurs in accordance with capacity and wills beyond capacity.

*1 Cor 13:5

36. Concerning the love* of God and neighbor, however, it is customary to doubt which of the two comes first. This is how it is determined. The love of God is one thing in beginning and another in having been cultivated. Indeed, people begin to love God before their neighbor, but since the love of God cannot be perfected unless it is fostered, and it grows through the love of neighbor, it is necessary that the neighbor be loved. Thus it follows that the love of God comes

**dilectio*

---

[129] *Minus amare proximum convincitur, qui necessitate cogente, necessaria non partitur.* The idea but not exact wording is found in Gregory's *Homiliae in Evangelia*, 20.11 (on Luke 3:1-11) (ed. Raymond Étaix, CCSL 141 [Turnhout: Brepols, 1999], 162; Hurst, trans., *Homilies*, 6:43): *Diliges proximum tuuum tamquam teipsum, minus proximum amare convincitur, qui non cum eo in necessitate illius etiam ea quae sibi sunt necessaria partitur.* The idea with that different wording is found in Bede, *In Lucae Evangelium Expositio* 3:11, in *Bedae Opera Pars II*, ed. David Hurst, 3; CCSL 120 (Turnhout: Brepols, 1960), 78–79, without attribution to Gregory. The 13th-century Albertus Magnus cites the idea in this different wording and as ascribed to Gregory, in *Commentariae in IV Sententiarum (Dist. I–XXII)*, d. XV, a. 16, ob. 5 (*Opera Omnia*, vol. 29, ed. Auguste Borgnet [Paris: Apud Ludovicum Vives, 1894], 494). It is also found in the early 14th-century *Manipulus florum*, compiled by Thomas of Ireland, ascribed to Gregory. For an English translation of Gregory's homily, see Homily 6 in *Homilies*, trans. Hurst, 35–49, esp. 43.

first as a beginning. It proceeds from the love of neighbor as needing to be fostered by it. And this is perfection in the love of God, that if the moment of necessity should occur, the person would die by whatever sort of death before transgressing one of the least precepts of God. Concerning love of neighbor, likewise, this is perfection: that one loves the enemy and would lay down his soul for his brothers. For thus it is written: *Love your neighbors, do good to those who hate you, pray on behalf of those who persecute and calumniate you,** and in another place, *Greater charity has no one, than to lay down his soul for his friends.**

*Matt 5:44

*John 15:13

37. Justly, therefore, charity is called a sign by which the elect are distinguished from the reprobate. For they cannot be distinguished by faith or generosity of alms or knowledge or fondness for fasts or vigils or martyrdom, for these are common to the elect and the reprobate. Thus only charity distinguishes the children of God from the children of hell,* for the Lord says, *In this will all know that you are my disciples, if you have love for one another.** Charity gathers the children of God and causes them to dwell in unity: *Behold how good and how pleasant it is for brothers to dwell in unity.** And in another place it is written, "Where charity and love are, there is the congregation of the saints. There is neither anger, nor indignation, but sure charity forever." [130] No virtue is strengthened without charity, but on the contrary each is destroyed in sin. For without charity the expert is foolish, and any ignorant people, if they have charity, are greatly learned, by the testimony of divine Scripture.* Those who hold char-

*see 1 John 3:10; Matt 23:15

*John 13:35

*Ps 132:1

*see 1 Cor 1:26-27

---

[130] *Consuetudines Marbacenses* 124.283, ed. Josef Siegwart (Freiburg: Universitätsverlag Freiburg Schweiz, 1965), 229. This appears to be an antiphon for the liturgical celebration of the Lord's Supper during the Holy Triduum. Just before the singing of this antiphon the choir is directed to recite Ps 132, *Behold how good* (124.282).

ity in their behavior hold both what is open and what is hidden in the divine sayings.

O, what might I appropriately recount about charity, which does not hide knowledge from the ignorant or satisfaction from the needy and does not deny medicine to the sick or protection to the healthy. Charity calls the predestined by an interior inspiration, justifies those called, and glorifies those justified.* It rouses the lazy that they might fight, supports the fighting that they might be victorious, and crowns the victorious that they might reign. It touches those puffed up by knowledge so that they might be humble and instructs those who are ignorant and lowly so that they might understand and be exalted.* It coaxes without flattery and is fierce without cruelty; with the weak it is weak, and it burns on behalf of the scandalized.* It does great things, and it does small things, so it is never idle. It rejoices in confessors, delights in virgins, burns hot in martyrs, and reigns in angels. In humble confessors it is redolent of a violet, in devout virgins it sprouts forth like a lily, in holy martyrs it reddens like roses,¹³¹ in blessed angels it shines like refined gold.*

O how sweet and beneficial is the bond of charity, as blessed Augustine affirms,¹³² in which the poor are

*see Rom 8:30

*see Luke 1:52

*see 2 Cor 11:29

*see Job 28:15;
Isa 13:12;
Dan 10:5

---

¹³¹ The same correlation of violets to confessors, lilies to virgins, and roses to martyrs is found in Ambrose, *Expositio evangelii secundum Lucam*, 7.128 (CCSL 14:258). See also Bernard of Clairvaux, SC 28.10 (SBOp 1:199; CF 7:97).

¹³² For reference to the "bond of charity" (*vinculum charitatis*), see Augustine, SS 209.3, 350.3, in *Sermons 184–229W*, and *Sermons 273–305A*, trans. Edmund Hill, The Works of Saint Augustine: A Translation for the 21st Century, vols. 3/6, 3/8 (Hyde Park, NY: New City Press, 1990); and *Homilies on the Gospel of John* 26.13, trans. Edmund Hill, The Works of Saint Augustine: A Translation for the 21st Century, vol. 3/12 (Hyde Park, NY: New City Press, 2009).

rich and without which the rich are poor![133] Charity sets limits in prosperity, endures in adversity, is most secure in temptation and most lavish in hospitality, most joyful among true brothers and most long suffering among false ones. It is free in Paul for the sake of censuring, humble in Peter for the sake of obeying, human in Christians for the sake of confessing, divine in Christ for the sake of forgiving.

38. Charity, therefore, teaches and works marvelous, beautiful, and best things. For it teaches that what ought to be loved should always be loved, so that what ought not to be loved might never be loved. Nothing that ought to be loved equally or less with regard to itself should be loved more; nor should anything be loved equally that ought to be loved less or more; nor should anything be loved less that ought to be loved equally or more.

All people ought to love only four things: God (of course), the angels, their own selves, and human beings. Things other than these must be loved minimally, but one ought to make use of them for a place and time, and the Creator must be praised for his creation and admired in these things. For instance, God and the neighbor must always be loved; however, sin must never be loved. Neither should the neighbor be loved more or less, but equally, although works of charity must not be rendered equally. Likewise, our bodies must be loved neither more than nor equally to our souls, but less.

39. Moreover, charity teaches men and women to rejoice with those who rejoice and to mourn with those who mourn,* to abstain from what is forbidden, to surpass what is permitted,* to give what is unnecessary, to share what is necessary, to love one's enemy,* to die for one's neighbor. Love purifies, illuminates,

*Rom 12:15
*1 Cor 10:23
*Matt 5:44

---

[133] See Augustine, S 350.3; Ps-Bernard here closely follows Augustine's interpretation, taking the entire last sentence of the paragraph directly from Sermon 350.

enflames, and strengthens the heart: purifies, I say, from the filth of sins, illuminates toward understanding, enflames to loving, and strengthens to working and persevering. Charity is the life of words and thoughts, the life of virtues and works, because each of these, if it does not sprout from the root of charity, does not live but is dead.[134] For charity is the life of the blessed souls, the life even of the angels, because neither souls nor angels live except by the charity of God, by which they are fed. Likewise, charity is the death of sins, the strength of those fighting, the palm of victors, which faith receives, toward which hope runs, and to which the accomplishment of all good works is subject.[135]

---

[134] This sentence represents the notion of charity as the form of the virtues. See the discussion on this point by Peter Lombard, *Sentences* III, d. 23, trans. Giulio Silano (Toronto: Pontifical Institute of Medieval Studies, 2008). In the *Summa Theologiae* II–II, q. 23, a. 8, Thomas Aquinas discusses whether charity is the form of the virtues. In the response to the second objection of that same article, where the objector quotes Eph 3:17, "Rooted and founded in charity," to make the point that charity is not the form but the matter of the thing—i.e., only the first part of virtue—Thomas writes, "Charity is compared to the foundation or root insofar as all other virtues draw their sustenance and nourishment therefrom, and not in the sense that the foundation and root have the character of a material cause." Charity as the root of all the virtues arises a few times in the *Summa theologiae*, twice in relation to the Ephesians passage. See I–II, q. 62, a. 4, obj. 1, and q. 65, a. 5, obj. 2. It also arises in other works by Aquinas, as in the *De virtutibus*, q. 2, a. 11, *ad* 5; *Contra retrahentes*, chap. 6, co., as well as in Thomas's commentaries on Scripture (*Super Matthaeum* [Reportatio Ledoegarii Bissuntini], chap. 13, I. 1; *Super Ioannem*, chap. 15, 1.2; and *Super II ad Corinthios*, chap. 12, I. 3).

[135] For a parallel see Julian Pomerius (or Ps-Prosper of Aquitaine), *The Contemplative Life* 3.13 (trans. Mary J. Suelzer, in *Ancient Christian Writers* 4 [Westminster, MD: Newman Bookshop, 1947]). There charity is described as "the death of crimes, the life of virtues, the strength of warriors, the palm of victors, the soul of holy minds, the source of good merits, the reward of the perfect."

*amor
‡dilectio

Charity, however, is not perfect unless fraternal love* is maintained with the love‡ of God: for whoever is separated from fraternal community is deprived of participation in divine charity.[136] Christ is God and man: therefore the one who hates a human being does not love the whole Christ. Although some appear to be participants by faith and good works, yet because they are deprived of fraternal love* they have no increase of virtue. As the apostle says, *If I speak with the tongues of men and angels but do not have charity, I am made as a sounding trumpet or ringing cymbal. And if I had known prophecy and learned all mysteries and all knowledge and had all faith, so that I might move mountains, but I do not have charity, I am nothing. And if I should distribute all of my riches to feed the poor and surrender my body so that I might burn but I do not have charity, it profits me nothing.*[137]* Indeed charity of all the virtues occupies the first place, whence it is also called *the bond** of perfection,*‡ because all the virtues are bound by her chain.

*dilectio

*1 Cor 13:1-3

*vinculum
‡Col 3:14

---

[136] This entire section from "for whoever is separated" up until "because all the virtues are bound by her chain" is a collection of quotations from the *Sententiae* of Isidore of Seville, 2.3 (CCSL 111:96–98). Ps-Bernard is probably quoting Isidore from the 9th-century compilation made by Smaragdus of Saint-Mihiel in *The Crown of Monks,* trans. David Barry, CS 245 (Collegeville, MN: Cistercian Publications, 2013), 4.

[137] The relation of fraternal love to the love of God is, as might be expected, a common theme in monastic authors including Bernard of Clairvaux, Aelred of Rievaulx, and William of Saint–Thierry. Though all of these have written extensively on charity (see especially Aelred's Spec car, William's *The Nature and Dignity of Love,* and Bernard's SC and Dil), the more frequent reference is to 1 Cor 13:4-8 rather than 13:1-3. Bernard, however, uses 1 Cor 13:1-3 while describing the twofold operation of the Holy Spirit (SC 18.6; SBOp 1:108; CF 4:138–39) and also makes many references to 1 Cor 12 and 13 in the course of his plea for peace in the monastic community (SC 29.3 [SBOp 1.204–5; CF 7:104–5]).

O how blessed is the virtue of charity, which embraces all, loves all, sustains all! It blots out sins, nourishes virtues, and, as is written, restrains anger, refuses hatred, drives out greed, hinders strife, and equally puts to flight all vices! Among reproaches it is untroubled, and in anger it is calm; amid hatred it is kind, and in truth it is firm; it is not despoiled by vicious attackers, by bandits it is not stolen, by fire it is not consumed, by heresy it is not divided. It stands indivisible, remains unconquerable, persists unshaken, and rejoices uncorrupted. Charity is harmony, the reward and fellowship of the elect.[138] *Charity is patient*, because it is not broken in adversity.[139] *Charity is kind*, because it devotes works of mercy to friends and enemies. *Charity is not envious*, because "it loves the good of another as its own"; *it does not act wrongly*, because it is not led to perverse work; *it is not puffed up*, because no prosperity lifts it up; *it is not ambitious*, because "it

---

[138] The whole passage from "O how blessed" is taken almost verbatim from the writings of Smaragdus of Saint-Mihiel. The passage appears to have been a central piece of Smaragdus's reflection on the virtue of charity, as it appears in almost the same wording in his *Via Regia* 2 (PL 102:937), *Commentary on the Rule of Saint Benedict* 4.21, trans. David Barry, CS 212 (Kalamazoo, MI: Cistercian Publications, 2008), and *The Crown of Monks*, 4. It should be noted that in Smaragdus's text the final phrase reads *concordia mentium, societas electorum* (the harmony of minds, and society of the elect).

[139] This entire passage is an extended exegesis of 1 Corinthians 13, which draws upon the interpretation of Peter Lombard, *In epistolam I ad Corintheos*, 13.3–9 (PL 191:1661). The portions of text in quotations identify the following borrowings: *alterius bonum diligit ut suum* / it loves the good of another as its own, *non vult aliis praponi* / it does not want to be put in front of others, *non provocateur ad iram* / it is not provoked to anger, *in actu pro veritate* / in act for truth, *quae veritas suadet* / which truth proposes, *in ipso capite, id est in Christo* / in the head itself, that is, in Christ, *quia etsi opera ejus cessent . . . nec in hoc saeculo, nec in futuro finitur* / even if its works should cease . . . is ended neither in this age nor in the future.

does not want to be put in front of others"; *it does not seek its own things,* because it sets communal things before its own and not its own before communal things. *It is not irritated,* because "it is not provoked to anger," and not only does it do no harm by work, but it does not think evil; *it does not rejoice over iniquity, but it rejoices together with truth, it bears all* "in act for truth"; *it believes all* "that truth proposes"; *it hopes for all* that truth promises, *it endures all,* "in the head itself, that is, in Christ." *Charity never fails,** because "even if its works should cease," nevertheless charity itself "is ended neither in this age nor in the future."

*1 Cor 13:8

Or charity in the elect does not fail, because, even if someone who is elect should sin criminally, charity in him still does not fail irrevocably. However, the one who preserves this virtue in works obtains blessing, as is confirmed by Scripture, which speaks thus to the people of Israel: *However, if you will hear so that you fulfill all of his commands, the Lord will make you higher than all the nations that dwell on the earth. You will be blessed in the field, and you will be blessed in the city. Blessed shall be the fruit of your womb, and blessed shall be the fruit of your land. The Lord will send forth blessing upon your cell*[140] *and upon all the works of your hands.**

*Deut 28:1, 3-4, 8

---

[140] The Latin word is *cellam,* which might also be translated "storeroom" or "cellar." This is a change from the standard wording of the Vulgate, which has *cellaria tua* (your storerooms). It seems likely that Ps-Bernard recognizes in the word an interpretative link to the monk's cell.

Bibliography

Primary Sources

Abelard, Peter. *Sic et non.* Ed. Blanche B. Boyer and Richard McKeon. Chicago: University of Chicago Press, 1977.

———. *Theologia Christiana.* In *Petri Abaelardi opera theologica,* edited by Eligius M. Buytaert. CCCM 12. Turnhout: Brepols, 1969.

Adam of St. Victor. "Sermon for the Feast of all Saints." In *Sacred Latin Poetry,* edited by Richard Chenevix Trench. 3rd ed. London: MacMillan, 1874.

Alan of Lille. *Dicta Alia.* PL 210:253–64.

Albert of Padua. *Sermo duodecimae dominicae post Pentecosten.* Paris, 1550.

Albertus Magnus. *Commentarii in II Sententiarum.* In *Opera Omnia,* edited by Auguste Borgnet. Vol. 27. Paris: Apud Ludovicum Vives, 1894.

———. "In IV Sententiae." In *Opera Omnia,* edited by Auguste Borgnet. Vol. 29. Paris: Apud Ludovicum Vives, 1894.

Alexander of Hales. *Summa theologica.* Nurenberg: A. Koberger, 1481.

Ambrose of Milan. *De patriarchis.* CPL 132.

———. *Expositio evangelii secundum Lucam.* CCSL 14.

———. *Expositio in psalmum 118.* CPL 141:467.

———. "Hexaemeron." In *Hexameron, Paradise, Cain and Abel,* translated by John J. Savage. FC 42. Washington, DC: Catholic University of America Press, 1961.

Anonymous of Einsiedeln. *Commentary on "O Qui Perpetua."* Ed. R. B. C. Huygens. CCCM 171:117–20. Turnhout: Brepols, 2000.

Anselm de Cantorbéry. *Pourquoi Dieu s'est fait homme.* Ed. and trans. René Roques. SCh 91. Paris: Éditions du Cerf, 2005.

Aquinas, Thomas. *Commentary on the Gospel of St. Matthew (Super Matthaeum).* 2 vols. Trans. Jeremy Holmes. Lander, WY: Aquinas Institute, 2013.

———. *Commentary on the Letters of Saint Paul to the Corinthians (Super II ad Corinthios)*. Trans. F. R. Larcher, B. Mortensen, and D. Keating. Ed. J. Mortensen and E. Alarcón. Lander, WY: Aquinas Institute, 2012.

———. *Commentary on St. John (Super Ioannem)*. 3 vols. Trans. James Weisheipl with F. R. Larcher. Albany, NY: Magi Books, 1980.

———. *Disputed Questions on Truth*. 3 vols. Chicago: Henry Regnery, 1952–1954.

———. *The Literal Exposition of Isaiah: A Commentary by St. Thomas Aquinas (Expositio super Isaiam ad litteram)*. Trans. Louis St. Hilaire. Steubenville, OH: Emmaus Academic, 2017.

———. *On the Virtues in General (De virtutibus)*. Trans. J. P. Reid. Providence, RI: The Providence College Press, 1951.

———. *Refutation of the Pernicious Teaching of Those Who Would Deter Men from Entering Religious Life (Contra retrahentes)*. Trans. John Procter. In *An Apology for the Religious Orders*. London: Sands and Company, 1902.

———. *Scriptum Super Libros Sententiarum*. Ed. R. P. Mandonnet. Paris: Lethielleux, 1929.

———. *Summa Theologiæ: Latin Text and English Translation*. 61 vols. 1964; Cambridge, UK; New York: Cambridge University Press, 2006.

———. "Super Euangelium Iohannis reportatio." In *Opuscula Theologica*, edited by R. Cai. Taurini-Romae: Marietti, 1975.

Aristotle. *Nichomachean Ethics*. Trans. Martin Ostwald. Indianapolis: Bobbs-Merrill, 1962.

Augustine of Hippo. *The City of God against the Pagans*. Ed. and trans. R. W. Dyson. Cambridge: Cambridge University Press, 1998.

———. *The City of God, Books 8–16*. Writings of Saint Augustine, vol. 7. Trans. Gerald J. Walsh and Grace Monahan. FC 14. Washington, DC: Catholic University of America Press, 1952.

———. *Confessionum libri XIII*. Ed. Lucas Verheijen. CCSL 27. Turnhout: Brepols, 1990.

———. *Contra Faustum*. Ed. Joseph Zycha. CSEL 25:251–797. Prague: F. Temsky, 1891.

———. *De bono conjugali* and *De sancta virginitate*. Ed. and trans. P. G. Walsh. Oxford Early Christian Texts. Oxford: Clarendon Press, 2001.

———. *De civitate Dei*. Ed. Bernard Dombart and Alphonse Kalb. CCSL 48. Turnhout: Brepols, 1955.

———. *De doctrina Christiana*. Ed. Joseph Martin. CCSL 32. Turnhout: Brepols, 1962.

———. *De Genesi ad litteram libri duodecim*. Ed. Joseph Zycha. CSEL 28/1. Vienna: Austrian Academy of Sciences, 1894.

———. *"De Genesi contra manichaeos."* In *On Genesis*. Trans. Roland J. Teske. Washington, DC: The Catholic University of America Press, 1990.

———. *De opere monachorum*. PL 40:547–82.

———. *De Trinitate*. Ed. W. J. Mountain. CCSL 50, 50A. Turnhout: Brepols, 1968.

———. *Enarrationes in Psalmos*. Ed. Franco Gori. CSEL 95. Vienna: Verlag der Österreichischen Akademie der Wissenschaften, 2010.

———. *Enchiridion on Faith, Hope, and Love*. Trans. J. F. Shaw. NPNF 1, 3. London: T&T Clark, 1883.

———. *Expositions of the Psalms 33–50*. Trans. Maria Boulding. The Works of Saint Augustine: A Translation for the 21st Century, vol. III/16. Hyde Park, NY: New City Press, 2000.

———. *Expositions of the Psalms 51–72*. Trans. Maria Boulding. The Works of Saint Augustine: A Translation for the 21st Century, vol. III/17. Hyde Park, NY: New City Press, 2001.

———. *Homilies on the First Epistle of John*. PL 35:1977–2062.

———. *Homilies on the Gospel of John*. Trans. Edmund Hill. The Works of Saint Augustine: A Translation for the 21st Century, vol. 3/12. Hyde Park, NY: New City Press, 2009.

———. *In Iohannis epistulam ad Parthos tractatus*. PL 35:2052.

———. *The Literal Meaning of Genesis*. Trans. John Hammond Taylor. Mahwah, NJ: Paulist Press, 1982.

———. *On Christian Doctrine*. Trans. D. W. Robertson, Jr. Indianapolis, IN: Bobbs-Merrill, 1958.

———. *"On Nature and Grace."* In *Four Anti-Pelagian Writings*, trans. John A. Mourant and William J. Collinge. Washington, DC: Catholic University of America Press, 1992.

———. *On Rebuke and Grace*. Trans. Robert Ernst Wallis. NPNF 5. Buffalo, NY: Christian Literature Co., 1886–1889.

———. *Sermones de novo testamento* (157–183). Ed. Shari Boodts. CCSL 41Bb. Turnhout: Brepols, 2016.

144   *Three Pseudo-Bernardine Works*

8——. *Sermons, 184–229W*. Trans. Edmund Hill. The Works of Saint Augustine: A Translation for the 21st Century. Vol. 3/6. Hyde Park, NY: New City Press, 1990.

——. *Sermons, 273–305A*. Trans. Edmund Hill. The Works of Saint Augustine: A Translation for the 21st Century. Vols. 3/8. Hyde Park, NY: New City Press, 1990.

——. *Tractates on John*. Ed. R. Willems. CCSL 36. Turnhout: Brepols, 1954.

Bede. *Commentaries on the Beginning up to the Birth of Isaac and the Casting out of Ishmael (Commentarii in Principium Genesis usque ad Nativitatem Isaac et Ejectionem Ismaelis)*. Vol. VII: *Commentaries on the Scriptures*. The Complete Works of Venerable Bede. 12 vols. Ed. J. A. Giles. London: Whitaker and Co., 1844.

——. *Homeliarum evangelii libri II*. CPL 1367.

——. *In Lucae evangelium exposito*. Ed. David Hurst. CCSL 120. Turnhout: Brepols, 1960.

——. *In primam partem Samuhelis libri iv. Nomina locorum*. CPL 1346.

——. *In principium Genesis usque ad nativitatem Isaac*. Ed. Charles Williams Jones. CCSL 118A. Turnhout: Brepols, 1967.

Beleth, John. *Summa de Ecclesiasticis Officiis*. Ed. Heribert Douteil. CCCM 41A. Turnhout: Brepols, 1976.

Bernard of Clairvaux. *Apologia ad Guillelmum abbatem*. SBOp 3:61–108.

——. *De consideratione*. SBOp 3:379–493.

——. *Five Books on Consideration: Advice to a Pope*. Translated by John D. Anderson and Elizabeth T. Kennan. Bernard of Clairvaux, vol. 13. CF 37. Kalamazoo, MI: Cistercian Publications, 1976.

——. *Liber de diligendo Deo*. SBOp 3:109–54.

——. *Liber de gradibus humilitatis et superbiæ*. SBOp 3:13–59.

——. *Monastic Sermons*. Trans. Daniel Griggs. CF 68. Collegeville, MN: Cistercian Publications, 2016.

——. *On Loving God*. Trans. Robert Walton. CF 13. Kalamazoo, MI: Cistercian Publications, 1995.

——. *Opera omnia*. Ed. Johannis Mabillon. Paris, 1839.

——. *The Parables and the Sentences*. Trans. Michael Casey and Francis R. Swietek. Ed. Maureen O'Brien. CF 55. Kalamazoo, MI: Cistercian Publications, 2000.

——. *Parabolae*. SBOp 6/2.

———. "St Bernard's Apologia to Abbot William," Trans. Michael Casey. In *The Works of Bernard of Clairvaux, 1.* Treatises I. CF 1. Spencer, MA, and Shannon, Ireland: Cistercian Publications, 1970.

———. *Sancti Bernardi Opera.* Ed. Jean Leclercq, C. H. Talbot, and H. M. Rochais. Rome: Editiones Cistercienses, 1957–1977.

———. *Selected Works.* Trans. G. R. Evans. New York: Paulist Press, 1987.

———. "The Sentences." In *The Proverbs and the Sentences*, translated by Maureen O'Brien. CF 55. Kalamazoo, MI: Cistercian Publications, 2000. 113–458.

———. *Sententiae.* SBOp 6/2.

———. *Sermones de Diversis.* SBOp 6/1:56–406.

———. *Sermones super Cantica Canticorum.* SBOp 1–2.

———. *Sermons on the Song of Songs.* Trans. Kilian Walsh and Irene Edmonds. 4 vols. CF 4, 7, 31, 40. Kalamazoo, MI: Cistercian Publications, 1976, 1979, 1980.

———. *The Steps of Humility and Pride.* In *Treatises II*, translated by M. Ambrose Conway. CF 13. Kalamazoo, MI: Cistercian Publications, 1980. 1–82.

Boethius. *De Consolatione Philosophiae.* Ed. Ludwig Bieler. CCSL 94. Turnhout: Brepols, 1958.

Bonaventure. "Commentarius in Euangelium sancti Lucae." In *Opera omnia.* Ad Claras Aquas (Quaracci): Collegii S. Bonaventurae, 1895. 7:1–604.

———. *Commentary on the Gospel of Luke, Part III, Chapters 17–24.* Trans. Robert Karris. New York: Franciscan Institute Publications, 2001.

———. "De purificatione b. Mariae Virginis." In *Sermons de diversis*, edited by Jacques Guy Bougerol. 2 vols. Paris: Editions Franciscaines, 1993.

Bruno the Carthusian. *Expositio in Psalmos.* PL 152:637–1420B.

Caesarius of Heisterbach. *Dialogus Miraculorum—Dialog über die Wunder.* Trans. Nikolaus Nösges and Horst Schneider. FC 86, vol. 5. Turnhout: Brepols, 2009.

Cassian, John. *De incarnatione Christi contra Nestorium haereticum.* Ed. Michael Petschenig. CSEL 17:233–391. Vienna: Verlag der Österreichischen Akademie der Wissenschaften, 2004.

Catherine of Siena. *Dialogue.* Trans. Algar Thorold. London: Kegan Paul, Trench, Trübner, and Co., 1907.

Cato, Dionysius. *The Distichs of Cato: A Famous Medieval Textbook.* Trans. Wayland Johnson Chase. Madison: University of Wisconsin Press, 1922.

Climacus, Johannes. *The Ladder of Divine Ascent*. Trans. Colm Luibheid and Norman Russell. The Classics of Western Spirituality. Mahwah, NJ: Paulist Press, 1982.

Conrad of Eberbach. *The Great Beginning of Cîteaux: A Narrative of the Beginning of the Cistercian Order: The Exordium Magnum of Conrad of Eberbach*. Trans. Benedicta Ward and Paul Savage. Ed. E. Rozanne Elder. CF 72. Collegeville, MN: Cistercian Publications, 2012.

Consuetudines Marbacenses. Ed. Josef Siegwart. Freiburg: Universitätsverlag Freiburg Schweiz, 1965.

Damian, Peter. "Carmina 40," in *Hymnus ad Sexta; L'opera poetica di S. Pier Damiani*, edited by Margareta Lokrantz. Studia Latina Stockholmensia 12. Uppsala: Almqvist & Wiksell, 1964.

———. *Sermones*. PL 144:505–924.

Durand, William. *Rationale divinorum officiorum*. Ed. A. Davril and T. M. Thibodeau. CCCM 140A. Turnhout: Brepols, 1998.

Expositio super septem libri apocalypsis. PL 17:765–970.

Gregory the Great. *Dialogues*. Trans. Odo John Zimmerman. FC vol. 39. Washington, DC: The Catholic University of America, 1959.

———. *Forty Gospel Homilies*. Trans. David Hurst. CS 123. Kalamazoo, MI: Cistercian Publications, 1990.

———. *Homiliae in Evangelia*. Ed. Raymond Étaix. CCSL 141. Turnhout: Brepols, 1999.

———. *Moralia in Iob*. Ed. Marc Adriaen. CCSL 143, 143A, 143B. Turnhout: Brepols, 1979.

———. *Moral Reflections on the Book of Job*. Trans. Brian Kerns. 6 vols. CS 249, 257, 258, 259, 260, 261. Collegeville, MN: Cistercian Publications, 2014–2020.

Guibert of Nogent. *Epistula Guiberti ad Lysiardum suessionensem episcopum*. PL 156:680B.

———. *Epistularium Guiberti: Epistulae Guiberti*. CCCM 66, 66A.

Hermann of Runa. *Sermones festivales*. Ed. Edmund Mikkers. CCCM 64. Turnhout: Brepols, 1986.

Hesbert, René-Jean, ed. *Antiphonale Missarum sextuplex*. Brussels: Vromant, 1935.

Hildegard von Bingen. "Liber diuinorum operum." Ed. Albert Derolez and Peter Dronke. CCCM 226. Turnhout: Brepols, 1996.

————. "O Clarissima Mater: Carmen 9." In *Opera Minora*, edited by Hugh Feiss, et al. CCCM 226. Turnhout: Brepols, 2007.

————. *Scivias*. Ed. Adelgundis Führkötter. 2 vols. CCCM 43, 43A. Turnhout: Brepols, 1978.

Hrotsvitha. "Abraham," in *Liber II*. In *Hrotsvithae Opera*, edited by Paulus von Winterfeld. SS rer. Germ. 34. Berlin: apud Weidmannos, 1902.

Hugh of St. Victor. *De Sacramentis*. In *Corpus Victorinum*, edited by Rainer Berndt. Aschendorff: Monasterii Westfalorum, 2008.

————. *On the Sacraments of the Christian Faith*. Trans. Roy Deferrari. Cambridge, MA: Medieval Academy of America, 1951.

Isidore of Seville. *De ecclesiasticis officiis*. Ed. Christopher M. Lawson. CCCM 113. Turnhout: Brepols, 1989.

————. *Sententiae*. Ed. Pierre Cazier. CCSL 111. Turnhout: Brepols, 1998.

————. "Synonyma de Lamentatione Animae Peccatricis." In *Isidore of Seville's Synonyms (Lamentations of a Sinful Soul) and Differences*, translated by Priscilla Throop. Charlotte, VT: MedievalMS, 2012.

Jerome. *Commentarii in prophetas minores*. Ed. Marc Adriaen. CCSL 76, 76A. Turnhout: Brepols, 1969, 1964.

————. *Commentariorum in Esaiam libri I–XI*. Ed. Marc Adriaen and G. Morin. CCSL 73A. Turnhout: Brepols, 1963.

————. *Commentariorum in Matheum libri IV*. Ed. David Hurst and Marc Adriaen. CCSL 77. Turnhout: Brepols, 1969.

————. *Dialogus adversus Pelagianos*. Ed. C. Moreschini. CCSL 80. Turnhout: Brepols, 1990.

————. *Liber de nominibus Hebraicis*. PL 23:771–858.

John of Salisbury. *Policraticus*. Ed. K. S. B. Keats-Rohan. CCCM 118. Turnhout: Brepols, 1993.

Julian Pomerius (= Ps-Prosper of Aquitaine). *The Contemplative Life*. Trans. Mary J. Suelzer. Ancient Christian Writers 4. Westminster, MD: Newman Bookshop, 1947.

Lawson, Ruth Penelope. *The Threefold Gift of Christ. By Brother Bernard. Translated and Edited by a Religious of C.S.M.V. [i.e. Sister Penelope] [A Translation of "Instructio Sacerdoti de Praecipuis Mysteriis Nostrae Religionis," Formerly Attributed to St. Bernard of Clairvaux]*. Fleur de Lys Series of Spiritual Classics 4. London: Mowbray, 1954.

Leo the Great. *Tractatus septem et nonaginta*. Ed. A. Chavasse. CCSL 138A. Turnhout: Brepols, 1973.

Naso, P. Ovidius. *Metamorphoses, Books 1–8.* Ed. Jeffrey Henderson. Loeb Classical Library no. 42. Cambridge, MA: Harvard University Press, 1984.

Origen. *On First Principles.* Notre Dame: Ave Maria Press, 2013.

Paschasius Radbertus. *De assumptione sanctae Mariae uirginis.* Ed. Albert Ripberger. CCCM 56. Turnhout: Brepols, 1985.

Pelagius. *Verba seniorum: Bk. 15. De humilitate.* PL 73:953–69.

Peter Lombard. *Commentarium in Psalmos.* PL 191:55–1296.

———. *In epistolam I ad Corintheos.* PL 191:1533–1696.

———. *Sentences.* Trans. Giulio Silano. Toronto: Pontifical Institute of Medieval Studies, 2008.

Peter the Cantor. *Verbum abbreviatum.* Ed. Monique Boutry. CCCM 196. Turnhout: Brepols, 2004.

Ps-Augustinus Belgicus. *Sermones ad fratres in eremo commorantes.* PL 40:1235–1358.

Ps-Dionysius, *The Mystical Theology and the Celestial Hierarchies.* Godalming, Surrey, UK: Shrine of Wisdom, 1949.

Ps-Venantius Fortunatus. *Symbolum Athanasianum.* Ed. B. Krusch. MGH auct. ant. 4.1. Berlin, 1885.

Rabanus Maurus Magnentius. *De universo libri viginti duo.* PL 111:9–614.

———. *Expositio in Matthaeum.* Ed. Bengt Löfstedt. CCCM 174. Turnhout: Brepols, 2000.

RB 1980: The Rule of St. Benedict in Latin and English with Notes. Ed. Timothy Fry. Collegeville, MN: Liturgical Press, 1981.

Richard of St. Victor. *Mysticae Adnotationes in Psalmos* 44. PL 196:321–24.

Rupert of Deutz [= Rupertus Tuitiensis]. *Commentaria in Canticum canticorum.* CCCM 26.

———. *De sancta trinitate et operibus eius.* Ed. H. Haacke. PL 167:197–1827. CCCM 21–24. Turnhout: Brepols: 1971–1972.

Sedulius Scottus. *Carmen Paschale.* CPL 1447.

———. "In euangelium Matthaei." In *Sedulius Scottus: Kommentar zum Evangelium nach Matthäus,* edited by Bengt Löfstedt. Freiburg im Breisgau: Verlag Herder, 1989.

Sicard of Cremona. *Mitralis de officiis.* Ed. Gábor Sarbak and Lorenz Weinrich. CCCM 228. Turnhout: Brepols, 2008.

Smaragdus of Saint-Mihiel. *Commentary on the Rule of Saint Benedict.* Trans. David Barry. CS 212. Kalamazoo, MI: Cistercian Publications, 2008.

———. *The Crown of Monks.* Trans. David Berry. CS 245. Collegeville, MN: Cistercian Publications, 2013.

———. *Diadema monachorum*, in *Opera Omnia.* PL 102:593–690.

———. *Vita Regia*, in *Opera Omnia.* PL 102:931–70.

Stephen of Bourbon. *Tractatus de diversis materiis praedicabilibus.* Ed. Jacques Berlioz and Jean-Luc Eichenlaub. CCCM 124, 124B. Turnhout: Brepols, 2002.

Sulpicius Severus, *De vita Beati Martini.* PL 20:159–76.

Tertullian. *Against the Jews.* CPL 33.

Thomas of Ireland. *Manipulus Florum.* Ed. Chris L. Nighman. *Electronic Manipulus Florus Project.* Waterloo, Ontario: Wilfrid Laurier University, 2004.

Vita Burchardi Episcopi. PL 134:507–36.

Voragine, Jacob. *Legenda aurea (vulgo Historia lombardinca dicta).* Ed. Johann Grässe. Osnabrück: Zeller, 1965.

William of Saint-Thierry. *Epistola (aurea) ad fratres de Monte Dei.* Ed. Paul Verdeyen. CCCM 88. Turnhout: Brepols, 2003.

Secondary Sources

Allen, Charlotte. "Thirteenth-Century English Religious Lyrics, Religious Women, and the Cistercian Imagination." PhD dissertation, Catholic University of America, 2011.

Anciaux, Paul. *La théologie du Sacrement du Pénitence au XIIᵉ siècle.* Louvain: E. Nauwelaerts, 1949.

Anderson, Gary A. *Charity: The Place of the Poor in the Biblical Tradition.* New Haven: Yale University Press, 2013.

Anderson, Luke. *The Image and Likeness of God in Bernard of Clairvaux's Free Choice and Grace.* Bloomington, IN: AuthorHouse, 2005.

Balnaves, Francis John. "Bernard of Morlaix: The Literature of Complaint, the Latin Tradition and the Twelfth-century 'Renaissance.' " PhD thesis, Australian National University, March 1997.

Bastiaensen, A. A. R. Toon. "Exorcism: Tackling the Devil by Word of Mouth." In *Demons and the Devil in Ancient and Medieval Christianity*, edited by Nienke Vos and Willemien Otten. Leiden & Boston: Brill, 2011. 129–42.

Bejczy, István. "De 'Formula vitae honestae' in het Middelnederlands: een bibliografisch wespennest." *Ons Geestelijk Erf* 78 (2004): 25–30.

Bell, David N. *The Image and Likeness: The Augustinian Spirituality of William of St Thierry*. CS 78. Kalamazoo, MI: Cistercian Publications, 1984.

Bestul, Thomas H. *Texts of the Passion: Latin Devotional Literature and Medieval Society*. Philadelphia: University of Pennsylvania Press, 2015.

Bloomfield, Morton W. *Incipits of Latin Works on the Virtues and Vices, 1100–1500 A.D.: Including a Section of Works on the Pater Noster*. Cambridge, MA: The Medieval Academy of America, 1979.

Breitenstein, Mirko. "*Consulo tibi speculum monachorum*. Geschichte und Rezeption eines pseudo-bernhardinischen Traktates (mit vorläufiger Edition)." *Revue Mabillon* 20 (2009): 113–49.

———. *Das Noviziat im hohen Mittelalter: Zur Organisation des Eintrittes bei den Cluniazensern, Cisterziensern und Franziskanern*. Vita regularis 38. Münster: LIT, 2009.

———. *De novitiis instruendis: Text und Kontext eines anonymen Traktates vom Ende des 12. Jahrhunderts*. Vita regularis 1. Münster: LIT, 2004.

———. "Der Traktat vom 'inneren Haus': Verantwortung als Ziel der Gewissensbuildung," in *Innovation in Klöstern und Orden des Hohen Mittelalters: Aspekte und Pragmatik eines Begriffs*, edited by Mirko Breitenstein, Stefan Burkhardt, and Julia Burkhardt. Vita regularis 48. Berlin: LIT, 2012.

Burch, George B. *The Steps of Humility by Bernard, Abbot of Clairvaux*. 3d ed. Cambridge, MA: Harvard University Press, 1950.

Butler, Cuthbert. *Western Mysticism*. London: Constable & Co., 1922.

Cavallera, Ferdinand. "Bernard (Apocryphes attribués à saint)." DSpir 1:1499–1502.

Chase, Steven, ed. *Angelic Spirituality: Medieval Perspectives on the Ways of Angels*. Mahwah, NJ: Paulist Press, 2002.

"Contrapasso." *The Dante Encyclopedia*. Ed. Richard Lansing. New York: Garland Publishing, 2000.

DelCogliano, Mark. "Cistercian Monasticism in the Silver Age: Two Texts on Practical Advice." CSQ 45 (2010): 421–52.

Delhaye, Philippe. "Dans le sillage de S. Bernard. Trois petits traités *De Conscientia.*" *Cîteaux* 5 (1954): 92–103.

Faithful, George. "A More Brotherly Song, a Less Passionate Passion: Abstraction and Ecumenism in the Translation of the Hymn 'O Sacred Head Now Wounded' from Bloodier Antecedents." *Church History* 82 (2013): 779–811.

Gilson, Étienne. *The Mystical Theology of Saint Bernard.* New York: Sheed & Ward, 1940.

Giraud, Cédric. *Spiritualité et histoire des textes entre Moyen Âge et époque moderne. Genèse et fortune d'un corpus pseudépigraphe de méditations.* Série Moyen Âge et Temps Modernes 52. Paris: Institut d'Études Augustiniennes, 2016.

Gondreau, Paul. *The Passions of Christ's Soul in the Theology of St. Thomas Aquinas.* Scranton: University of Scranton Press, 2009.

Hamm, Berndt. *Promissio, Pactum, Ordinatio: Freiheit und Selbstbindung Gottes in der scholastischen Gnadenlehre.* Tübingen: Mohr Siebeck, 1977.

Janauschek, Leopold. *Bibliographia Bernardina qua Sancti Bernardi primi abbatis Claravallensis operum cum omnium tum singulorum editiones ac versiones, vitas et tractatus de eo scriptos quotquot usque ad finem anni MDCCCXC reperire potuit.* Xenia Bernardina 4. Vienna: Hölder, 1891.

Jansen, Katherine Ludwig. "Maria Magdalena: *Apostolorum Apostola.*" In *Women Preachers and Prophets through Two Millennia of Christianity,* edited by Beverly Kienzle and Pamela J. Walker. Berkeley and Los Angeles: University of California Press, 1998. 57–96.

Javelet, Robert. *Image et ressemblance au XIIᵉ siècle, de saint Anselme à Alain de Lille.* 2 vols. Paris: Éditions Letouzey & Ané, 1967.

Jorissen, Hans. *Die Entfaltung der Transsubstantiationslehre bis zum Beginn der Hochscholastik.* Münster, Westfalen: Aschendorffsche Verlagsbuchhandlung, 1965.

Kitanov, Severin Valentinov. *Beatific Enjoyment in Medieval Scholastic Debates: The Complex Legacy of Saint Augustine and Peter Lombard.* Lanham, MD: Lexington Books, 2014.

Lachance, Paul. "Introduction," in *Angela of Foligno: Complete Works.* Trans. Paul Lachance. Mahwah, NJ: Paulist Press, 1993.

Ladner, G. B. *The Idea of Reform.* Cambridge, MA: Harvard University Press, 1959.

Leclercq, Jean. "Introduction to Saint Bernard's Sermons *De diversis.*" CSQ 42 (2007): 37–41.

———. "Introduction to the Sentences of Bernard of Clairvaux." CSQ 46 (2011): 277–86.

———. "La préhistoire de l'édition de Mabillon." In *Études sur Saint Bernard et le texte de ses écrits.* ASOC 9 (1953): 202–25.

———. "Le premier traité authentique de Saint Bernard?" RHE 48 (1953): 196–210. Reprinted in Jean Leclercq, *Recueil d'études sur saint Bernard et ses écrits.* Rome: Edizioni di Storia e Letteratura, 1966. 51–68.

Madigan, Kevin. *The Passions of Christ in Medieval Thought: A Essay on Christological Development.* Oxford: Oxford UP, 2007.

McGuire, Brian Patrick. "Cistercian Storytelling—A Living Tradition: Surprises in the World of Research." CSQ 39 (2004): 281–309.

Mellinkoff, Ruth. *The Horned Moses in Medieval Art and Thought.* Berkeley: University of California Press, 1970.

Newhauser, Richard. *The Treatise on Vices and Virtues in Latin and the Vernacular.* Turnhout: Brepols, 1993. 55–96.

Newhauser, Richard, and István Bejczy. *A Supplement to Morton W. Bloomfield, et al., Incipits of Latin Works on the Virtues and Vices, 1100–1500 A.D.* Turnhout: Brepols, 2008.

Rouse, Mary A., and Richard H. Rouse. *Preachers, Florilegia and Sermons: Studies on the* Manipulus florum *of Thomas of Ireland.* Toronto: PIMS, 2000.

Rubenstein, Jay. *Guibert of Nogent: Portrait of a Medieval Mind.* New York: Routledge, 2002.

Schulte, Augustin Joseph. "Viaticum." *The Catholic Encyclopedia.* New York: Robert Appleton Company, 1912.

Sicard, Patrice. Iter victorinum. *La tradition manuscrite des œuvres de Hugues et de Richard de Saint-Victor. Répertoire complémentaire et études.* Biblioteca Victorina 24. Turnhout: Brepols, 2015.

Titus, Craig Steven. *Resilience and the Virtue of Fortitude: Aquinas in Dialogue with the Psychosocial Sciences.* Washington, DC: Catholic University Press, 2006.

Wilmart, André. "Grands poèmes inédits de Bernard le clunisien." RBen 45 (1933): 249–54.

———. *Le Jubilus dit de Saint Bernard.* Storia e Letteratura 2. Rome: Edizioni di Storia et Letteratura, 1944.

Scriptural Index

Scriptural references in all three works are cited by numbered paragraph and/or note.

BAdmon: Brief Admonition; Form: *Formula honestae vitae*; Inst: *Instructio sacerdotalis*; n.: note; Pref: Preface; Tract: *Tractatus de statu virtutum*

Genesis

1:2	Tract Pref
1:26	Inst 1; Tract 17, n. 49
1:26-27	Inst n. 16
2:8-9	Tract 16
2:16-17	Tract 22
2:17	Tract 16
3:5	Inst 8
3:8	Tract n. 52
3:19	Form 4
4:2-4	Inst 22
14:18-20	Inst 22
18:12	Form n. 13
22:1-18	Inst 22
22:18	Inst 3
28:12	Tract 13, n. 39
29:17	Inst n. 66
32:30	Tract n. 52

Exodus

3:1-6	Tract 23
4:10	Tract 23
4:13	Tract 23
6:9	Inst 10
12	Inst 22
19:12-13	Inst Pref
33:11	Tract n. 52
33:18-23	Inst 17
33:20	Inst 17
34:29-30	Tract n. 69
38:8	Inst 28

Deuteronomy

4:24	Inst 16
6:5	Inst 14
10:16	Inst 7
28:1	Tract 39
28:3-4	Tract 39
28:8	Tract 39
30:6	Inst 7
30:14	Inst 32
34:10	Tract n. 52

1 Samuel

14	Tract n. 57
14:24-46	Tract 19
15:22	Tract 26, n. 91
24:15	Tract 11

2 Samuel

6:22	Tract 11

1 Kings

13:11-28	Tract 19
13:24	Tract n. 57

2 Kings

23:25	Inst 14

Job

1:1	Tract n. 114
7:1	Inst 8
9:28	Form 8
20:6-7	Tract 3